To Set One's Heart

BELIEF and TEACHING in the CHURCH

Sara Little

John Knox Press
ATLANTA

Library of Congress Cataloging in Publication Data

Little, Sara.
  To set one's heart.

  Includes bibliographical references and index.
  1. Christian education.   2. Faith.   I. Title.
BV1471.2.L56   1983   207   82-49020
ISBN 0-8042-1442-5

© copyright John Knox Press 1983
10 9 8 7 6 5 4
Printed in the United States of America
John Knox Press
Atlanta, Georgia

Preface

This is a book about teaching, basically. But when I think about all the concerns and expressions of some of my own core beliefs that are gathered here, I recognize that the book is more than that. Nonetheless, it is developed in the context of the church and the church's teaching ministry, and what is viewed as a need to take a next step in that ministry. A long tradition of distinguished thinkers is represented today by persons like Ellis Nelson and Randolph C. Miller and John Westerhoff, who focus on the community of faith as the matrix for the emergence and development of faith. That tradition is affirmed and assumed here. But certain factors in the present situation, in both church and society, call for attention to belief. Thus teaching presents itself for consideration.

The book moves through an analysis of belief and makes a case for an approach to teaching that deliberately focuses on the formation and re-formation of belief and belief systems. In the process, there is an opportunity to say a word to those who set faith over against belief, teaching over against liberation or socialization or transformation, and thinking over against feeling or even becoming. Those small battles will be of most interest to educational theorists, who probably will not change their minds after reading the book, anyway. The more important thing, however, is my conviction that in these days the whole concept of intentionality in teaching, developed in terms of carefully formulated approaches, can help us think together and work together to contribute to various facets and levels of belief. *Something* is claimed for teaching, but it is viewed as part of a whole ministry, and not as everything, as an answer to all problems facing the church. My hope is that pastors, educators, and all those persons seriously engaged in linking theory and practice, theology and psychology and sociology, will be among those to respond to the invitation to join together in developing a *paideia* for today.

At one point, I thought this book began with a 1978 Yale-Berkeley-Hartford Conference on "The Future of Educational Ministry" where I gave a paper on "Belief and Behavior." It took on form and substance during my 1979 sabbatical from Union Theological Seminary in Virginia, a time for which I am indebted to Union, especially to Fred Stair and Neely McCarter, then President and Dean, respectively. Certainly I need to mention a few of the groups and occasions which have contributed to my thinking: the David Nyvall Lectures at North Park Seminary, the Rice Lectures at Nazarene Seminary, the Johns Lectures at Memphis Theological Seminary, the Presbytery of the Cascades 1981 Conference on

"How Faith Becomes Real" (people are still sending clippings, ideas, even poems, from Oregon). There have been courses which helped me in the early stages of my work, at Princeton Theological Seminary, and Presbyterian School of Christian Education, and then one at Union in January 1982 where student-colleagues stimulated enough new insights that I wanted to start over. Conversations with persons like Charles Melchert of the Presbyterian School of Christian Education, and Denham Grierson of United Theological Faculty in Melbourne, Australia, bring forth the same response, along with gratitude. But in spite of all these excursions into belief, I discovered to my amazement when I had occasion to review earlier writings that I have spent much of my life working on the meaning of "to set one's heart." That recognition became especially clear as I was rereading portions of *The Language of the Christian Community*.

One other matter: Neely McCarter (formerly of Union, now President of Pacific School of Religion) should have been co-author of this book. In our thinking and teaching, our ideas became so intermingled that it would be impossible to separate them—especially in our response to Kierkegaard, Bruner, Buber, Freire, and Dewey. How could I say how much he has contributed to a kind of "symphonic awareness" of meaning for me? And there have been others who have contributed, too—many others, especially Sally Hicks and Mickey Lumpkin. But this preface must stop sometime.

Sara Little
Union Seminary, Richmond

Contents

Dedicated to my sister
HELEN

1

The PRESENT SITUATION

"Let not many of you become teachers," New Testament writer James said. He was right, because, as he added, "you know that we who teach shall be judged with greater strictness."[1] Teachers, by teaching, accept the responsibility of seeking to know and increasingly to appropriate the truth they seek to teach, as well as the responsibility of trying to develop those structures and processes which in themselves witness to the truth, and enable those who learn to receive, to build knowledge, to respond with others in faithfulness, and to be transformed by the meaning they find. There are other reasons, too, to approach teaching with an attitude of hesitant questioning. But there are also compelling reasons to *try* to teach, and to locate at least some clues as to the direction the church might take in its teaching ministry if it considers seriously its responsibility in this area for this present moment in history.

In order to deal more directly and thoughtfully with some of those clues to be proposed, consider first some of the problems and possibilities confronting the church and church teachers today. Look at the yearning need to believe of people inside and outside the church as a possible starting point for locating a direction, and then reflect on an organizing center for that direction and a formulation of a relationship between believing and teaching. Themes introduced in this overview or context will be explored in greater depth in succeeding chapters.

Is teaching necessary or desirable?

Issues emerging out of a reflection on James' warning about teaching multiply rapidly as one thinks about personal responsibility, the ethics of methodology, the disciplined thought and work necessary to give form to vision, the potential "corrupting" power of success, and the debilitating results of "failure," or the danger of becoming immune to the sacred by "handling" it repeatedly. However, these are perennial issues. They have faced teachers for centuries, and there is no sign that they will disappear. They have to do with the teacher's beliefs, attitudes, and integrity. Moreover, they have to do with the values shaping the culture of the institution and society which the teacher represents—values which shape the teacher through the culture, and yet are to be called in question by that same teacher.

The issue in that last sentence leads one to a question about the relationship of teaching and the socializing forces of culture (both secular and religious). At that point, one is faced with a recurring issue which does have particular importance for the church's teaching ministry in this latter part of the twentieth century. That issue has seldom been posed more precisely than by Dwayne Huebner. He asks, ". . . is education in a religious community necessary or is living religiously with others inherently educational?"[2] He even raises the question of whether we need to "attend to education" if we focus on "being religious with others." Several writers and teachers in the current church education scene (maybe even the majority, in fact) build their theory around the conviction that the faith-life of the religious community and its worship and work are what is important. Influential John Westerhoff, a prolific writer, develops this theory with attention to a variety of facets of "living religiously with others," with special interest in worship; for him, "to attend to education," at least in part, is to prepare for worship, to relate liturgy and learning. For the others, the church functions as conscience to the world in its embodiment of the prophetic voice, or becomes a nurturing community supporting people in crisis and personal maturing. Whatever the focus, the beliefs and values *experienced* in the community are "learned," so that it is fitting to raise a question about the value of education, and even urgent to ask whether teaching is necessary.

In exploring the matter, an immediate reaction is to say that it is impossible to think of "handing on the faith" apart from the community of faith. In Hebrew life, whether it was through a story told about the campfire, the role of an individual in the tribe, the question "Why?" asked at the table, or the deeds of justice, mercy, and love, education occurred because of and through that community. At no point in the Christian history can it be said that educational systems or intentional teaching could survive, be understood, or be effective apart from the life of the community.

Ellis Nelson summarizes the matter in his *Where Faith Begins,* assuming the faith community, but going beyond its life to a broader context and more comprehensive process, still centered in the community. As he sees it,

> My thesis is that faith is communicated by a community of believers and that the meaning of faith is developed by its members out of their history, by their interaction with each other, and in relationship to the events that take place in their lives.[3]

Although almost all of his book is devoted to interpreting his thesis, Nelson does recognize preaching and teaching as "more deliberate efforts of the Christian community to form the mentality of its members."[4] He gives limited attention to developing the idea, but ends the book with a call for a "new deliberateness" about what is communicated and how it is communicated, recognizing the difficulties of effecting change.

A second reaction to the issue about "being religious" versus education, then, is to inquire whether it is possible deliberately to intervene in the process of transmitting values, and if it is, where the forms of that intervention might legitimately be called education or teaching. A study of Greek history and philosophy is informative at that point. In his monumental three-volume *Paideia: Ideals of Greek Culture,* Werner Jaeger reflects on the decline of Greek political power and internal societal structures that occurred during the fourth century. In the gloom and sense of impending disaster of that period, "the great geniuses of education" appeared.[5] Socrates, although chronologically of the fifth century (469–399 B.C.) was the intellectual turning point leading to the age of Plato, when Socrates' thought became influential. This fourth century, with its turmoil and change, "is the classical epoch in the history of paideia, if we take that to mean the development of *a conscious ideal of education and culture.* "[6] Concerned to find a way to understand and reform their culture, "all the energies of thinking men were concentrated" in attention to ideals and ideas, along with systems, programs, and aims which could shape culture and mold character.[7] These great philosopher-educators are not to be viewed as rationalists dealing only with intellectual abstractions. Their thoughts and acts are to be understood—as is always the case—in relationship to their history. Activities of power or force could not "save" Athens; only truth could. Thus, "it is in the bitter but magnificently enthusiastic struggle to determine the nature of true paideia that the real life of the period finds its characteristic expression,"[8] and as a result, although the nation was not preserved from destruction, the inheritance of the thinkers is still available to the world, to new generations who still try to preserve and reform by persuasion and power. It is because "the will to make the highest powers of the spirit contribute to building up a new society was never more serious and more conscious than in this age,"[9] that the fourth century B.C. is cited. This twentieth century A.D. may be—in fact, is—quite different in many respects, but it is also a time of transition, even of crisis. The belief that education does make a difference, that matters of truth and meaning of the spirit—religious matters, if you will—are of basic importance, should confront the church with a need to explore with a "new deliberateness" the possibilities of teaching, which *is* both necessary and desirable. What will be offered here is only a particle, a fragment, that by its very incompleteness calls to be expanded into explorations of major scope.

"Onlooks"

What directions and constraints shall be placed on this "necessary and desirable" teaching to be undertaken by the church? The concept of "onlooks" introduced by Donald Evans is useful in reflecting on that question. *Faith, Authenticity, and Morality* is an investigation of the meaning and interrelationship of the three subjects designated in the title. In that investigation, Evans employs "onlooks," that is, "attitudes whose linguistic expression has, or can be, the form 'I look on *x* as *y.*'" For example, "I look on my life as a game (or a struggle, or a search, or a voyage, or a dream, or a drama, or a pilgrimage)."[10] The view is that one can assume some kind of understanding of what "game" is, and therefore, by analogy, can gain insights into the meaning of "life." What is produced is an attitude, a way of perceiving which deepens understanding and involves a predisposition to a particular kind of action. Evans develops the concept in a fascinating and sophisticated kind of way, using three types of "onlooks," and illuminating Christian faith in a new way. With respect to moral decisions, he sees "onlooks" as offering "an imaginative moral insight which combines 'is' and 'ought' in seeing that *x* is sufficiently like *y* to be treated like *y.*"[11]

It would be rewarding to employ Evans' methodology in a way that included teaching in the categories he investigates, but that would be another project. At this point, let us consider only one "onlook" and explore several implications embodied in it.

I look on teaching in and by the church as a form of ministry intentionally directed toward helping persons seek and respond to truth.

Ministry is a form of service, a person's response of gratitude to God's gracious action and being. Therefore teaching is always done as a responsive activity; it is never a matter of seeking control. What the teacher does is also to seek truth, to risk giving expression to what is perceived, but always in such a manner that the freedom of the student is not obstructed. Neither teacher nor student creates truth, nor is free to flout it. Theirs is a freedom to come to know it, to exercise all powers of intellection and volition and understanding in responding to it.

The fact that the church is the agency in and through which the teaching ministry takes place is important, too. As Evans says, "To be a Christian is to share in onlooks common to the Christian community as one understands that community."[12] But these "onlooks" are in a sense a suggestion of how one "ought" to view the world, and are a beginning point for struggles toward depth in authentic Christian faith. Here again, then, attitudes relating to church, ministry, and truth set directions and pose limits. Ultimate truth means being related to that which transcends the human, to God. It gives perspective, a frame of reference for all knowledge, even seemingly inconsequential details. Serving somewhat the same function as Evans "onlooks," paradigms, a more comprehensive term, may be developed as patterns by which we understand reality and perceive meaning, interpreting and relating events and ideas. Some such process of finding meaning is what is involved in "helping persons seek and respond to truth."

A key assumption, perhaps not made explicit in the "onlook," is that to be human is to need to perceive meaning in life. It is suggested in ideas just stated about paradigms and seeking truth. Michael Polanyi, philosopher-scientist concerned with meaning and ways of acquiring "personal knowledge," suggests that "we do not accept a religion because it offers us certain rewards." He goes on to say this: "The only thing that a religion can offer us is to be just what it, in itself, *is:* a greater meaning in ourselves, in our lives, and in our grasp of the nature of all things."[13] We can conclude that because teaching is concerned with truth and with helping persons, it is concerned with meaning. Because the church, as the community of faith, embodies meaning, teaching can help persons become conscious of the meaning found there. James Nelson, Christian ethicist, who sees the faith community as the "moral nexus" within which Christian identity is developed and moral decisions made, cites Horace Bushnell's sermon on "Unconscious Influence," joining Bushnell in the suggestion that we need to become more conscious of those "unconscious influences" that shape us.[14] That statement brings us back full circle to where we started in our analysis of the present state of the church's teaching ministry, and of needed directions for the future. What has been added, essentially, is the conviction that we need not only to develop categories by which we can interpret unconscious influence, but also to intervene in that influence by helping persons develop beliefs which inform and reshape the cultures of church and society. Moreover, we need to be more deliberate in our approach to helping persons claim the Christian inheritance in such a way that they can come to know who they are and why they are. Teaching, then, as an intentional activity, may be employed as an instrument for use by the church in helping persons find meaning in a chaotic world.

"Homelessness of mind"

All the way through the reflections on the present situation in the church and its teaching ministry, there has been a kind of running dialogue with the present situation in the world. Just as fourth-century Greece responded with new attention to paideia, so the "homelessness of mind" characteristic of most of the twentieth-century world calls for renewed attention to the human need for clarity about belief, about meaning. Direct attention to that need should produce some insights as to the focus appropriate for today's teaching ministry.

There are many factors that combine with the vacuum in belief and the confusion about what belief is to cause the "homelessness of mind" cited by sociologists Peter Berger, Brigitte Berger, and Hansfried Kellner as characteristic of the present era. In *The Homeless Mind,* as they analyze what is happening to people in the process of modernization, they see that people live in so many "life worlds," so many structures, that more and more individuals experience life as "migratory, ever-changing, mobile," with one "world" contradicting another. And religion seems unable to fulfill its function, "to provide ultimate certainty amid the exigencies of the human condition," so that " 'homelessness' has become metaphysical."[15] In a special study on the sociology of belief, James T. Borhek and Richard F. Curtis confirm this analysis, implying that many people

who experience deeply the "fractionated aspects of . . . existence" have no
"home" either to hold things together or to give support.[16]

The kind of need we are considering emerges in a particularly acute fashion
just now, manifesting itself in many different ways. His own "long preoccupation
with fragmentation and wholeness," says sociologist Robert Bellah, is what "has
made religion such an abiding concern" for him.[17] Reviewing his own life, Bellah
tells about his traditional Presbyterian background, and his excursion into Marxism in search of an ideology that would provide an "integrative role" for him.
Finding, instead, "a strait-jacket," he goes on to tell of his current reclaiming of
"the self-critical, self-revising, non-totalistic aspects of the tradition." He says,
"With respect to Christianity, this meant Christ crucified, the assertion of faith
in spite of the brokenness of every human structure."[18] Bellah seems to be talking
about faith more than about belief. He is among the social scientists who see
belief as more Western and provincial than universal in its importance for
religion, according to Martin Marty, and who are sympathetic with the wholistic*
approach of Eastern or primitive religions.[19] That search for wholeness seems to
be the universal element, and even if belief does not appear in cognitive form
in all religions, it *does* appear in the Western traditions, including the Christian.
Therefore in any case it is important for many people. Bellah himself is a clear
example of an intellectual in search of a home. True, for Bellah or for anyone,
when belief is equated with religion or supersedes faith, when it becomes a
control mechanism or a test for salvation, it is a prison rather than a home.

In addition to the need for "home" with respect to belief and belief systems
is the need for clarity and even passionate commitment where leadership is
concerned. Contending that there is a kind of vacuum in leadership at the
present, David Loye, a social psychologist, says that in the long span of history,
leaders usually had a clear sense of direction, consistent with and even based on
what they believed. They were "in love with the idea," he says, quoting Bertrand
de Jouvenel.[20] Both their goals and their leadership styles were fashioned according to their ideology. Contrasted to this significant kind of belief system is the
shallow, uninformed, and uncommitted opinion or attitude.

Further, the present situation calls for people who are willing to *think.* What
we are talking about is both thinking as a component in believing, and thinking
in response to the moral decision-making in an increasingly complex society. Few
people pose the need more convincingly than Hannah Arendt, philosopher-
teacher who took up residence in the U.S. after escaping Nazi Germany. In the
Introduction to her Gifford Lectures, published as *The Life of the Mind,*[21] she
comments that her "preoccupation with mental activities" came from several
sources, most immediately from attending the Eichmann trial in Jerusalem. In
her report of it, she refers to "the banality of evil." What struck her, she says,

---

*Connoting "wholeness," this spelling is preferred to "holistic" and is used throughout the book.

was the "manifest shallowness in the doer" (Eichmann)—not the demonic nature of his motives, but rather his *"thoughtlessness."* Helpless when routine procedures did not exist to guide his responses, he used "cliché-ridden language" and gave no evidence that he knew how "to *stop* and think." The question raised for her is this: "Might not the problem of good and evil, our faculty for telling right from wrong, be connected with our faculty of thought?" She says she does not intend to suggest "that thinking would ever be able to produce the good deed as its result," but rather that the habit of thinking might be "among the conditions that make men abstain from evil-doing or even actually 'condition' them against it." This possibility is only one of the philosophic issues she pursues in her rewarding study, but a reader gains the impression that Hannah Arendt's deep concern for people and their lives is behind her rejection of "stock phrases" and "standardized codes of expression and conduct." For her, events and facts, just "by virtue of their existence," make a claim on the thinking attention of people. This is partly what it means to be human, as expressed through the "thinking, willing, and judging" activities that constitute "the life of the mind."

Belief is not the same thing as thought, and believing is not the same thing as thinking. But thought is surely a major component in belief, as belief is in faith. Note that belief is multi-layered, that it has affective (feeling), volitional (willing), and behavioral (acting) components, as well as cognitive (thinking). More precise analysis is postponed to the next chapter. Here it is important to note that belief is closely related to faith, that faith is the basic Christian or religiously important category, and that one of our concerns will be the relation of belief to faith. We hear so much about "faith" these days that we may neglect an important factor in faith—belief—as either flowing from faith, or feeding into, deepening and clarifying faith. This assumed close connection between belief and faith suggests that we are not dealing with superficial attitudes nor isolated facts. Our "belief" is closer to what Spanish philosopher Jose Ortega y Gassett meant with his reference not to "ideas which we *have,* but ideas which we *are."*[22] In fact, the term *credo,* translated from early creeds as "I believe," literally means "I set my heart."[23] *That* kind of believing is the focus of our concern in this book.

"Faith asking the intellect for help"

Hannah Arendt translates the often quoted statement of Anselm of Canterbury, *fides quarens intellectum,* usually expressed by "faith seeking understanding," as "faith asking the intellect for help."[24] This felicitous phrase captures a major need in this later part of the twentieth century. There have been times over and over in history when faith has "asked the intellect for help"—times of new scientific discoveries, and times when God has not only been proclaimed dead but experienced as dead. The knowledge explosion today raises questions of meaning. New areas in which ethical decisions must be made confront persons of faith with questions about what is believed. Too many conversations seem more like a collection of "You know's" piled on top of each other than like the use of language to clarify thought. With the phenomenal development of religious sects and groups,[25] one observes a kind of seeking for security and an uninformed trust in exploitative leaders—a kind of formless faith, as it were, all pointing to the need for reflection. Indeed, if there is validity in Hannah Arendt's intuitive question as to whether there may be a link between non-thought and evil, we may have one more clue as to what happened in Guyana with James Jones and the People's Temple.

Some of the illustrations may point not so much to the need for the intellect to serve faith as for the intellect to manifest its existence and to fulfill its own intrinsic nature. Another way of approaching the same idea is to say that part of what it means to be human is to have a mind and to use it. John Leith, Presbyterian theologian, says this: "What cannot be thought through critically and expressed with reasonable clarity cannot demand the allegiance of man's whole being."[26] Thus, he says, understanding is linked to commitment, and "faith must be spoken and made intelligible."[27]

What is being proposed here is not a call for a new Age of Reason. There is always danger that reason may slip from the servant role to become the master, full of pride and power.[28] What is called for is precisely what Anselm sees in the relation between faith and understanding. Jewish philosopher Abraham Heschel says that human motives for learning or understanding are threefold: "The Greeks learned in order to comprehend. The Hebrews learned in order to revere. The modern man learns in order to use."[29] Perhaps what the contemporary person who is Christian needs is to recapture the Hebrew heritage of awe and reverence. But there is something akin in the Greek heritage, though arising from the context of philosophy rather than faith. One answer to the question, "What makes us think?" is Plato's saying that "the origin of philosophy is Wonder."[30] Such thinking is surely inextricably intertwined with both believing and faith.

But a warning is in order. A look at history immediately calls to mind the misuse of belief, or the perverted belief that burns heretics for *their* beliefs, that sets correct doctrine or tests for orthodoxy as the essence of religion, that equates acquiescence or inherited belief with internal transformation. There have been times when emphasis on logic has outweighed the search for meaning, or show of knowledge has obliterated the risks of living with mystery.

There are other things to remember about the role of belief, however. The great fourth and fifth century creed-making period of the church, in spite of all the divisiveness that sprang from the effort to clarify doctrine, opened areas that are still of concern. Then consider the Reformation. Philip Schaff, scholar known best for his work on creeds, says that "The Reformation of the sixteenth century is, next to the introduction of Christianity, the greatest event in history."[31] Robert Bellah would not attribute to belief the importance that Schaff does, although his own analysis suggests that particular Reformation beliefs have functioned in a formative way and are of significance for him personally. He says this:

> The Reformation, especially in its Calvinist and sectarian forms, reformulated the deepest level of identity symbols, which as in all traditional societies were expressed as religious symbols, in order to open up entirely new possibilities of human action. God's will was seen not as the basis and fulfillment of a vast and complex natural order that man must largely accept as it is—the conception of medieval Christianity as of most traditional religion—but as a mandate to question and revise every human institution in the process of building a holy community.[32]

What a powerful way to summarize a belief, and to demonstrate the importance of "faith asking the intellect for help"!

A thesis

How, then, are we to understand and carry out the teaching task for the church in these next years? Terms like intentionality, respect for the learner, and responsibility to understand and interpret a subject suggest some such definition of teaching as this: Teaching is that offering on the part of the designated teacher of a structure and a process within which the intentional learner may be exposed to the integrity of the subject and supported in his/her efforts to understand and assimilate the meaning of that subject for himself/herself. This definition refers to teaching in general. It assumes that the teacher must be secure enough in knowledge of the subject area to know what approach to take to expose a learner to "the integrity of the subject," but that exposure may also be an occasion for the teacher's learning. When the definition is related to the "onlook" of that teaching, it takes on the added dimension of dealing with the integrity of the subject as being faced with the constraint and power of truth itself, ultimate truth. Teacher and student (really, companion pilgrims), stand before Truth, together, and there they find meaning, meaning for which people today desperately yearn.

Such an approach is based on the assumption that belief is important for us today, and belief formation is an appropriate organizing center for the church's teaching ministry.

Questions then come quickly. What *is* belief? What kinds of belief are there? *How* should beliefs be held? What can the church do? What can be done, specifically, in the church's teaching ministry?

The plan here is to work through these questions, generally in the order given. Underlying all these explorations is a thesis:

> *Beliefs which engage the thinking powers of the person as they emerge out of and inform faith, sustained, reformed, and embodied by the faith community, can be an important factor in bringing integration and integrity to*

life. Teaching that contributes to the formation of this kind of belief necessitates the selective use of a variety of models with clear purposes, and presupposes the existence of a context that supports and interacts with intentional teaching.

Notice the restraint of the language chosen. Beliefs can be "an important factor." No exorbitant claims are made here that one kind of emphasis in the life of the church and education will solve all problems. It should be obvious that we are working toward a particular kind of belief—not overbelief, not what Hans Küng calls "lofty dogmas" which even "keepers of the Holy Grail . . . can scarcely make intelligible to modern man."[33] All presuppositions could not be stated in the tightly knit thesis—for instance, that other things may be more important than teaching, but that teaching, carried out in an intentional way, can make a more effective contribution than it is presently doing. Another presupposition is that the faith community exists in a broader community, and experiences or events in that broader community make an impact on religious institutions or groups. Therefore behavior and experience interact with development of belief. But all this should become clearer as the thesis is developed, and as we move toward consideration of particular approaches to teaching.

2

The NATURE
and FUNCTION
of RELIGIOUS BELIEF

Some problems

Belief is not the same thing as faith. Nor is it to be equated with truth nor knowledge nor propositional statements. Yet is is related to each of these. When one thinks of the centuries philosophers have spent on concepts of truth and of knowledge, or theologians and biblical scholars have spent on these and concepts of faith as well, not to mention the more recent involvement of social scientists, one gets a hint as to the difficulties of comprehending belief. Philosopher H. H. Price begins his distinguished Gifford lectures entitled *Belief* with this statement: "Belief is a large and complicated subject."[1] He proves his point, and in the process moves through the complexity of belief to an affirmation of its necessity and value.

Difficulties of understanding arising from philosophical issues are compounded by shifts in the way the word *belief* has been used historically. When we delve into the whole Indo-European family of languages, including Old English and Middle English, as well as Latin and Germanic derivatives, and then investigate the Hebrew and Greek variations of words, all of these sources feeding into the noun *belief* or the verb *believe*, we cover a varied spectrum of meanings: to profess; to accept a statement as valid or true or authoritative; to think, expect, have an opinion, have a conviction; to love, desire, cherish, trust; that which is firm, reliable, certain, unfailing (like a tent peg fastened in a secure place).[2] Such a fascinating etymology could well be a book in itself. It points not only to sources for confusion, but also to depth and richness of meaning. Even in what is referred to here, we can see the strand that leads into the dominance of objective intellectual propositions or dogma, an emphasis that calls forth the criticism that religion is distorted when it is described only by beliefs. We can also see the strand that links belief to faith, in an attitude of trust. In fact, historian of religion Wilfred Cantwell Smith, in his *Belief and History*, says that "the idea that believing is religiously important turns out to be a modern idea,"[3] and that "the concept is not in the Bible."[4] What *is* there is the concept of faith. Because the original meaning of belief or believe was so close to that of faith, and because English has no verbal equivalent to go along with the noun-concept faith, the verb was translated as "believe." In the early church, belief and faith were not far apart in substance. Whatever definition of belief is to be used, then, must certainly take into account the relation of faith and belief.

Even in the present situation, either there are many meanings for the word *believe,* or there is a general carelessness about what is meant—perhaps both. Consider some examples. You are invited to dinner, and the hostess offers you a second helping. "May I serve you some asparagus casserole?" she says. You reply, "I believe not." What you actually mean is, "No, thank you." And everybody knows that. Someone calls, asks for Mary, and when he learns she is not at home, says, "Will she be at the basketball game?" "I believe so" is the reply. What that means is, "I'm not sure," or "I don't know." But everybody knows that. The caller may waste his time if he goes to the game expecting to find Mary there. In these instances, *belief* seems to be about halfway between opinion and knowledge, more than a guess but less than actual knowledge. The amount of certainty varies, and determines the point at which belief emerges on the continuum between opinion and knowledge.

Complicate the matter further. You are in a conversation about public schools. One person says, "I *think* public schools are in trouble these days." Another says, "I *feel* public schools are in trouble"; another, "I *believe* public schools are in trouble." It would seem, surely, that more careful use of language is possible to communicate whether the reaction is one of feeling or thinking. Or it may be that this third statement simply expresses the uncertainty of opinion, as in earlier illustrations. It would have been possible to say, "I believe *in* public schools," and thereby to combine components of both thinking and feeling, to say, in effect, "I think public schools have something to offer, that they are the arena for learning in a pluralistic society, and that we have an obligation to support them. Furthermore, I *care* what happens in our schools." This caring for "our" schools bears within it a predisposition to act. The last statement, with "believing *in*" rather than "believing *that,*" involves the whole person. What we have is a noun and a verb that, even when used carefully, may mean any one of several things, and may involve one or several or all of the human faculties or domains—the intellect, the emotions, the will, the behavior. All the relationships cannot be delineated, of course, but as we move toward a working definition or concept, one that fits the thesis with which we move to a consideration of teaching, we can at least be aware of the complex area in which we are working.

Belief and belief systems

Most people who have done extensive work on belief do not view all beliefs as alike. There are different levels, different types. Explorations into three approaches bring helpful insights.

Milton Rokeach, social psychologist who has spent a lifetime investigating the nature of belief systems, writes about three regions of the person in which beliefs are located—the central, the intermediate, and the peripheral—and about five types of belief.[5] Primitive belief, in the central region, is built up out of the earliest experience of the child about the nature of the physical world and of people. Primitive Type A is that belief in which society joins, about which there is consensus. One does not have to spend time analyzing or questioning. A table is a table. My mother is my mother. Primitive Type B is different. It also depends on direct encounter with the object of belief, but does not have the "taken for granted" nature of Type A beliefs that are shared and supported by external authority. There is zero consensus. Type B beliefs include both "pure faith" (a mother whose son could do no wrong) and phobias. A child, sometimes for reasons that never become clear, comes to a perception of the world as a hostile place, and feels, "I am an unlovable person." Even though contrary views exist elsewhere, the child is psychologically closed to them. In the intermediate region of the person, we find the third type, authority beliefs—beliefs developed on the basis of family and community, and of what reference groups and persons are accepted as authoritative. They are linkages between primitive beliefs and the expanding world of the growing person. In the peripheral region, the fourth and fifth types of belief develop—derived and inconsequential beliefs. Derived beliefs may be unexamined beliefs accepted because of assumed authority (the *Encyclopaedia Britannica*) or because of ideological beliefs related to institutions with which one is associated. They may grow out of more basic beliefs or experiences. Inconsequential beliefs, matters of taste, for example, border on not being beliefs at all. Yet they may be held with intensity.

Although there are many beliefs, organized according to the central-peripheral continuum, those most significant for the development of the person are the primitive beliefs, or what Rokeach sometimes calls nuclear beliefs. They are the ones most resistant to change, the ones that give cohesiveness to the belief system.

For James Dittes, Yale professor of psychology of religion, belief is the reproduction on the conceptual plane of inner reality.[6] Beliefs manifest themselves, and become accessible to us, as inferences about what is going on within. They are therefore indicators rather than springs capable of generating and guiding energies. He cites "the Calvinist conviction that what is visible is derivative,"[7] and distinguishes between "visible" beliefs and those inner "processes and postures and passions" like faith which "are powerful and generative and efficacious."[8] Different types of belief have different relationship to these inner postures. All three types are recognizable. Belief as *idol* binds energies and narrows perspective. It is external to the person, who serves and protects the belief. Belief as *saying* is located on the edge of a person's consciousness; it is casual, mindless, passionless. Belief as *index* is the "indicator" which is central to Dittes' view of belief. Developed and functioning in different ways even in two people, the "index" brings to the rational plane those subrational or transrational postures which shape the person.

If belief is no more than an indicator of other forces which have shaping power, one asks, why should we deal with belief at all? Precisely because belief *is* more accessible. Although it can never be a surrogate for faith nor for religion, although it is "a latecomer to the process of the person's and the culture's orientation and location and identification in the universe," it is nonetheless "an essential part of that process, essential to refining and testing and consolidating and anchoring and bounding that orientation." Or, to put it another way, "once the 'beliefs' are formulated, they in turn have their effect."[9]

Thomas Green, philosopher, sees belief—at least "core beliefs"—as more intrinsic to the being of the person than does Dittes. His core beliefs are more like Rokeach's primitive or nuclear beliefs in their constitutive power, more like Dittes' views in their focus on conceptualization. They are the "ideas which we *are*" of Ortega y Gassett, to which reference has already been made. They "define our most fundamental features of personality."[10] Held with passionate conviction, a core belief is one with "such psychological strength and regarded as so important and basic that it is not easily subject to investigation or dispassionate discussion."[11] Core beliefs move out into clusters of beliefs, and clusters into peripheral beliefs. They do not constitute logical systems, although relation between beliefs may be logical, with derived beliefs depending on primary beliefs, often within clusters. As systems, they are related psychologically and quasi-logically, sometimes with conflicts or no connections between clusters or levels.[12] People "have an incredible capacity to hold strongly to beliefs that are inconsistent," he says, which makes it possible, for example, so to isolate economic beliefs from ethical convictions that we never permit them to touch one another.[13] There are inconsistencies in clusters of beliefs. It is even possible to have conflicting core beliefs.

Green's interest is in teaching, "an activity which has to do, among other things, with the modification and formation of belief systems."[14] More about his view of teaching comes later. Here it is important to note that the number of core beliefs should be minimized. As a person "holds more and more beliefs as core beliefs, there will be fewer and fewer areas of inquiry open to him."[15] The rigidity of the closed person with complete conviction based on numerous core beliefs is no less lamentable than the complete openness of the vacillating person whose "placid and weak mentality marks him off as dangerous because he thinks nothing is really very important."[16] Neither can learn. On the other hand, the person who has a limited number of core beliefs has a beginning point for organizing, assimilating, and dealing with new ideas, and can therefore be open to learning. Green's concern is that teachers work on these "enabling beliefs," as much aware of *how* beliefs are held as of *what* is the content of the beliefs.

Obviously there is no consensus as to what belief is or how it is developed. Perhaps the different interests and disciplines of the persons studied account for that fact to some extent. With them, and with many other scholars, however, there seem to be at least three points of agreement with respect to the way belief can be viewed in the present.

First of all, belief has a strong cognitive component. It has to do with thinking, with understanding, with the use of words as tools and with efforts to enable thought to inform language and deed.

Second, the objective form in which beliefs become manifest as ideas or expressed values has a subjective content in which belief is rooted and through which it integrates cultural influences and individual activities and existence.

Third, the belief of any person must be understood both psychologically and historically. That is to say, it must be understood in context. Wilfred Cantwell Smith says that the statement "the sky is a cow" is a quite different statement from "the ancient Egyptians held the sky to be a cow."[17] The first points to the isolation of belief as an intellectual abstraction, an absurdity or falsehood. The second, although Smith himself says that he does not fully understand it, signifies harmonious rapport with nature and two thousand years of meaning symbolically communicated through poetry and art.

Acknowledging these three areas of agreement as qualifying the view of belief to be assumed for this study, let us go on to a fourth area, suggested before but made explicit by sociologists James Borhek and Richard Curtis. A belief, to be of any significance, must be a component in a belief system.

> *A belief system is a set of related ideas (learned and shared) which has some permanence, and to which individuals and/or groups exhibit some commitment.* [18]

Implicit in this quotation is a definition of belief as an idea which meets the conditions of some degree of permanence, commitment, and connectedness. The formulated content of that to which we give assent with at least a measure of force, vividness, and vitality parallels an inner activity of believing, a kind of introspective awareness of our own mental stance.

Borhek and Curtis add another condition to belief when they say that, for belief systems to serve human purposes, they must be perceived as *true*. They must

> . . . appear to group members as a suprasocial set of eternal verities, unchangeable through mere human action and agreed upon by all rightthinking people not because they (the verities) belong to a people but because they are TRUE.[19]

Unless beliefs are viewed as true, they become dysfunctional. The same authors add another connected point. Belief must not only be viewed as true, it must be confirmed as true. When it no longer serves to bring clarity to life, its usefulness is over. That is, "for commitment to persist the belief system must be validated."[20] And it must have internal coherence.

Summarized, this fourth condition qualifying our approach to belief suggests that belief, to be of value, must be a part of a belief system that is *adequate*.

What understanding of belief, then, is to serve as reference for this study? What is the "belief," assumed as a part of a belief system, to which these conditions apply? In a concise though perhaps overly simplified way, we could say that *a belief is an idea held (thought and experienced) to be true.*

Up to this point no distinction has been made between belief and religious belief. Reviewing what has been said, we would doubtless agree that what has been presented in general terms is applicable to religious belief. Some would say that nothing else is necessary, that religion has to do with the meaning in all experience, and that belief is inevitably religious because it is in fact formulation that is the interpretation of meaning. But the position taken here is that religion has to do with transcendent reality and one's response to it. Christian beliefs therefore have to do with the Christian faith tradition, or with probing beneath seemingly non-religious ideas to inquire about their ultimate significance. They have to do with the relating of oneself and one's world to the Christian God. In the massive *Research on Religious Development,* four dimensions of religion are isolated for research: beliefs, experience, practices, and behavior.[21] Of course religion cannot be so compartmentalized. These dimensions and others interrelate. But beliefs, momentarily pulled out for reflection, make sense only in the context of the whole of the lives of Christians in community. They make sense only in relation to the reality of faith.

Faith and belief

Pulling together and examining what has been said or assumed throughout this study, let us consider three affirmations about the relation of faith and belief.

First of all, faith *is* the religiously important category, and is not the same thing as belief. It would be hard to find anyone to quarrel with that statement. David Tracy, in his analysis of contemporary theology in *Blessed Rage for Order,* says this:

> . . . I am employing the familiar distinction between "faith" as a basic orientation and attitude (primal and often non-conceptual) and "belief" as a thematic explication of a particular historical, moral, or cognitive claim involved in a particular "faith" stance.[22]

That distinction is the one used here. Faith has a way of involving the whole person that is difficult for Westerners to understand. David Myers, in his psychological exploration of the relation of belief and behavior, *The Human Puzzle,* says that in Hebrew anthropology, persons "think with their hearts, feel with their bowels, and their flesh longs for God."[23] All of these human activities are an integral part of faith. Further, in the New Testament, especially in the writings of Paul, faith as a kind of inner condition is not an independent, static, spiritual or psychological quality, but is an orientation always related to the object of faith, God, whose faithfulness and steadfastness are essential for the possibility of faith.

Within that relationship, the person is formed and re-formed into the likeness of the object of faith.[24] Faith *is* a trust, loyalty, confidence, but it is more than a "feeling." It is a trust qualified by the One who is trusted. It is, in fact, a gift from that One who reveals himself. In that revelation and response, where faith is established as the relationship between God and his people, we have the uniqueness of what is known as Christian faith.

Beliefs then become avenues by which we reinterpret and thereby reappropriate at deeper levels the meaning of the Christian faith—meaning which becomes reality and not formulations about reality.

Beliefs are not the only avenues, of course, especially for some ages where belief in the technical sense is not possible. Cognitive development is still in too early a stage. But participation and identification with the faith community and the faith-full person *are* possibilities; they are the matrix out of which belief emerges. We shall look at such points more closely in the next chapter.

Second, the relation between faith and belief is reciprocal or interactive or correlative. It is not competitive. Indeed, there are points at which faith and belief seem to merge, especially when we distinguish between belief *that* and belief *in*. To believe *in* God or truth or justice is far more than a fleeting opinion or intellectual assent. It is near to Thomas Green's core belief of formative "passionate conviction" or Milton Rokeach's primitive belief. When one says, "I believe in Jesus Christ," trust and commitment are being expressed, or faith is being evidenced. To say, "I believe in John," or some other person, is to express faith in John. And unless individuals are "believed in," unless they can "believe in" others, the possibility of becoming *persons* is limited. *Who* is believed in and *what* is believed in are of ultimate importance. If the continuum from belief *that* to belief *in* merges with faith, then we have a kind of justification for dealing with belief.

What is said here is a kind of elaboration of what was said in our thesis, that belief emerges out of and in turn informs faith. It is consistent with Dittes' view that belief is "derivative," that it has to do with "refining and . . . anchoring" our orientation. For a Christian to say "I believe in Jesus Christ" may be an "idol" or a "saying" unless there are accompanying "beliefs that." Behind that simple affirmation, if it is made with understanding, is a wealth of documentation. The whole Judaic-Christian tradition, composed of many specific facts, concepts, beliefs, is pulled together in that focused, short sentence, and related to the existential situation of the speaker.

For David Tracy, working out his theological methodology, there are two principal sources for theology—Christian texts and common human experience and language. And they must be "related."[25] Interesting, is it not, how close are some of the approaches to "doing" theology (using a faddish term) and "thinking about" education? Some of the conditions or qualifying characteristics of beliefs specified here as appropriate for us in education are not far from Tracy's criteria for reflections on human experience (meaningfulness, meaning-as- internal-coherence, and truth or adequacy) and on Christian texts (appropriateness of interpretation). Theological content is developed from the correlation of these two sources.[26] Surely this is akin to the process of relating belief *in* and belief *that*, or faith and belief.

Briefly and unapologetically, in the third place, to look at belief as a factor in faith is to affirm the existence of a cognitive component. It is not the only component, and belief itself is not exclusively cognitive. But this moment is a good time to consider anew the cognitive process if some of the prevalent "homelessness of mind" is to receive attention, and if we are to respond to what Martin Marty calls the "new romanticism about non-cognitivity," which he says is actually an inaccurate rendering of what belief has basically been in the Western tradition.[27] Not many religious educators have expressed concern with "belief" in recent writings, in spite of the prolific works on faith. But that is a side comment. The primary interest here is in inviting educators to join with those in numerous other disciplines in their growing concern with belief. Even Wilfred Cantwell Smith, whose historical study of belief raises many searching questions, ends his *Belief and History* with an affirmation of the importance of ideas in human history. He adds this:

> It matters enormously that we find a proper belief to elucidate our faith. Part of that awesome austerity, that demand, that terror of which I speak, is the demand laid upon us to pursue the truth and to formulate it conceptually—as an inescapable obligation, yet secondary to the prior truth that precedes: the reality to which all propositions are subordinate.[28]

Functions of Christian belief systems

Minute listings of functions are possible, but for purposes here, general statements are adequate to provide a context for later consideration of the teaching ministry. Four functions of belief systems stand out.

To help a person make sense of the world and have a frame of reference for understanding, caring, deciding, and doing

The thinking, feeling, willing, acting person benefits from having a "mental home." The person as a whole, body, mind, and spirit, is influenced by and can lead a more integrated existence because of belief—*if* the belief is of a particular kind, an "enabling belief." Each human activity is influenced by that belief. And belief itself is reshaped by those activities. Core beliefs or primitive beliefs are reshaped only at great cost, with reverberations throughout the person. It is to be hoped, therefore, that beliefs can be developed in such a way that drastic or traumatic shifts are unnecessary, and that core beliefs can serve as filters or organizing centers for free inquiry and growth. Developing belief, if completed and confirmed in all human activities, can offer the much-needed help requested of the intellect by faith.

It is difficult to build the kind of belief system we are assuming. We rationalize our behavior and develop beliefs to protect it. To illustrate, reflect on the comment of a thoughtful young girl in an eleventh grade religion class in a private school, as the discussion centers on the relation between belief and behavior.[29] "But what about times you *do* something and then want to make yourself *think* it's right, so you say you believe something that makes the action right? Then the next time, you use that belief to do wrong again, and the belief gets stronger." Others agreed, and cited instances in our history where we have developed beliefs to justify what might be called immoral action.

The illustration brings up the question of motivation, and the eleventh grader's insight reminds one of Gordon Allport's comments. He says that the extrinsically religious person is motivated by "utilitarian, self-serving" purposes, and "uses" both God and religion. The intrinsically motivated person's religion is "interiorized" and lived out in an authentic unity of belief and behavior.[30]

In spite of all the difficulties, if there is any degree of integrity to the belief system, the person benefits. Dittes summarizes:

> My believing can signify (1) my feeling more in touch with, less subdued by complexities of the world; (2) my feeling more in touch with others who are "in the know"; (3) my feeling more in control of disruptive inner passions; (4) my feeling responsive to the data of reality; (5) my feeling responsive to, congruent with the perceptions of those whose perception of me is important to me; (6) my feeling the resolution of inner turbulence; and my sense that all of the above gains are sustained by the support of (7) the world, (8) other people, and (9) my own response.[31]

To aid a community—in our case, specifically the religious community called the church—to achieve identity and maintain continuity

This second function can be fulfilled because there is a relative permanence of the belief system, though not in the sense of fixed or static, but permanent in the sense of enough continuity for the "holy community" always in process of being reformed to recognize and participate in the continual reformation of belief.

In his classic *Treasure in Earthen Vessels,*[32] James Gustafson speaks of the church as a community of language and interpretation, of memory and understanding. Without the "common memory" of the church, individuals lose the sense of "roots," of identity, of direction. Language becomes important. As Paul Tillich suggests, when we lose a word, we lose the reality to which the word points. Moreover, language, as a channel for communication, must be used faithfully if it is to serve its purpose. As the expression of belief, it becomes a constitutive force in both communal and personal existence.

Although we are referring to belief and its role in the identity and continuity of a faith community, it is important to remind ourselves, with our explorations here, that other activities are also essential in the achievement of this function—worship, ritual, service, and the "plausibility structures" through which a community's actions and values embody and give rise to or reinforce belief.

To link human experience and the Christian tradition through an interpretation that internalizes meaning and gives direction to life

Implicit in this function is an assumption about one approach to "learning" and assimilating theology, consistent with the two main sources of theology of David Tracy. The kind of learning we are seeking is an internalized and transformational knowing. It is as John Calvin said:

> Doctrine is not an affair of the tongue, but of the life . . . [and] is received only when it possesses the whole soul, and finds its seat and habitation in the inmost recesses of the heart. . . . To doctrine in which our religion is contained we have given the first place, since by it our salvation commences; but it must be transfused into the breast, and pass into the conduct, and so transform us into itself, as not to prove unfruitful.[33]

If this function is to be fulfilled, there must be a community in which *together* people work through the kind of process of interpretation implied here. Not that a person cannot think alone. As Hannah Arendt sees it, in fact, there is a great need for thinking individuals who know what solitude is. She refers to the Socratic soundless dialogue which "I carry on with myself" ("the Two-in-One"): "The partner who comes to life when you are alert and alone is the only one from whom you can never get away—except by ceasing to think."[34]

But dialogue within oneself presupposes dialogue with others. The insight and support of others of the community of faith is necessary if meaning is to be formulated and internalized. James Gustafson is instructive here, in another of his books, *Can Ethics Be Christian?*

> One is born into and nourished in communities which provide interpretations of human experiences, and interpretations of the transcendent, the Holy, which is the object that evokes human response.[35]

Sometimes those interpretations or affirmations become "moments of personal appropriation . . . consent to its rightness . . . 'making sense' in one's own life." When that happens, not only is meaning internalized, thus shaping the attitudes and beliefs of the person, but the articulation of meaning becomes "construing belief, an orientation and direction within all of human experience."

To link lives of individuals and communities to larger, ultimate realities and purposes

From the perspective of the Christian tradition, the individual and the community are both incomplete, apart from the transcendent. When systems incorporate beliefs about transcendent reality, perceived as true, this fourth function has its basis.

One important point about this function is the emphasis it places on the importance of the *content* of what is believed. We have already considered the shaping power of the relationship when a person believes in something or someone. To believe in falsehood or to believe in one who is untrustworthy is to link one's life to the unworthy and the destructive. Truth is of ultimate importance. Some theorists hold that ideologies are usually socially invented or conditional responses to the environment, particularly the economic and cultural, foisted upon communities as a surrogate for religion or as a superstructure to obscure the lack of rationality in the world.[36] This is the kind of situation where the term ideology takes on pejorative overtones. It is a contrast to a belief system or ideology based on an interpretation of that reality which originates from beyond a human agency and draws persons to link their lives to ultimate purposes which have the persuasive power of Truth itself.

A second point has to do with the fact that thought and language are essential to the linkage of life and ultimate purpose. Contained within the language of the Christian community is the witness to our common memory. Through the language and the memory by which the community and the individual achieve identity and continuity, there is also the possibility for thinking together. We are not only nourished in the community, but we have within it the instruments for reflecting together about our own calling—in our language, our beliefs, always to be viewed as dynamic, not static. We have the words by which we seek together to understand, to make ethical decisions, to formulate a direction. In the process, not only is past linked to present and future, as in the third function of belief systems, but also—and that is the focus for this fourth function—transient human experience is brought into relationship with that which is transcendent and eternal.

These functions may seem like dreams, with more qualification and boundaries than will ever be possible to work through. Yet even to see the possibilities is to move in the direction of actualization. How do we go about that next step?

3

TEACHING and the CONTEXT of BELIEF

How does a person come to hold an idea as true? That is to say, how does a person come to believe? To develop a belief system? Is there some special kind of teaching that will lead to belief formation? The quick, emphatic answer to that last question is "no." There are some ways of teaching that are more effective than others, some appropriate for one purpose, some for another. But to the degree that teaching is a planned, intentional educational activity—and that is the sense in which it is being used here—it is a functional part of something else. In order to consider those first questions, or the relation of teaching to belief formation, therefore, we must look at that "something else," the context which, according to our stated thesis, "supports and interacts with intentional teaching." Maintaining wholistic perspective is difficult, but if we can work through some of the facets of the context, we should end up with a clearer view of both limitations and possibilities of teaching. First, then, we explore the context, including cultural, institutional, and personal factors, and later consider some observations about teaching.

Participation in the faith community

Suppose a young person of about age twelve were to have studied baptism, its historical origins, its biblical usage, and its creedal interpretations, and to have arrived at clear ideas which could be verbalized in ways that even knowledgeable adults would admire. But suppose that person, by some quirk, had never witnessed a baptism, never shared in a worship where baptism reminded the congregation of its organic unity, and had not been baptized. What had been verbalized might be informational only, not a belief "held to be true." Or if it were belief, it would likely be what Rokeach calls authority belief. The experience of participation in a community of faith where baptism has deep, pervasive, complex meaning relating to a whole system of belief is essential if one is to hold belief that even approaches the significance of reality.

The situation is obviously exaggerated. It is far more likely the case that a person might be baptized, view numerous baptisms, and move through an order of worship without understanding. In either case, the point should be clear. The church, with its tradition, is the context that gives meaning to baptism. The experienced reality is to be understood if meaning is to be clear and grow, and if it is to be internalized.

What we are thinking about here is the sociological concept that "out-of-context beliefs are meaningless."[1] James Borhek and Richard Curtis use this terminology to say that a belief must be understood in a context of meaning if it is to make sense. That is, baptism is a part of the Christian belief *system*. By implication, the same terminology is applicable to the structures through which baptism is enacted and experienced, to the social organization and the meaning it conveys. Baptism makes no sense apart from the rituals of the church, the worship and life of the community of faith. What is being said by these two sociologists is that beliefs are not intelligible apart from two social contexts, one of meaning, the other of organization.[2] The implication for teaching beliefs in their connectedness with one another and with the system of which they are a part leaps out at once. The implications for teaching of the institutional or organizational context is less obvious but equally important.

"Plausibility structures," as Peter Berger calls them, point to an important proposition of sociology of knowledge—that the views of reality that people find credible actually depend on "the social support these receive," both in structures that uphold and social consensus that reinforces those views.[3] Thus plausibility structures both support and enact the meaning of stated beliefs. Without them, even a tightly knit, logical system of beliefs could not sustain teaching about baptism or about any isolated doctrine. Recognition of that fact is important on at least two counts. On the one hand, a person collects ideas and impressions in an informal learning through participation in structures and processes. Even names of committees convey something—something that can be utilized more deliberately in the linkage of ideas that one studies with the practices of the church. On the other hand, at a deeper level, a teacher develops a kind of stance or orientation from this "social context" perspective. The inheritance which derives from and through that context is the source of the content to be thought and learned as it is reformulated and appropriated by both teacher and learner.

Understanding

How does individual reflection—a basic concern in our analysis of belief—relate to participation in the community? Stephen Toulmin is particularly helpful at this point. In his philosophical investigation in *Human Understanding,* he says that the human being is born with "the power of original thought," but "this originality is constrained within a particular conceptual inheritance." Viewed by some as "chains," these concepts, to the contrary, "turn out to be the necessary instruments of effective thought."[4] In his affirmation that communal aspects of language and shared concepts are presupposed for the possibility of personal or individual articulation of thought and belief, Toulmin makes enculturation basic for concept-acquisition. It is important to note, however, that what is basic is not a limit. In each new generation, "our conceptual inheritance is re-created," and persons have responsibility to criticize "particular forms of life and understanding . . . seeking to improve on them and working beyond them to better forms." The results will be "not merely products of a cultural process but also expressions of our native capacities."[5]

For theologian-educator Randolph Crump Miller, participation in the faith community provides the social contexts of meaning and organization, and makes available the conceptual inheritance necessary for human understanding. More important, for him and for others who share his position, is the *experience* of participation.[6] It is not so much that one is "socialized into" language and ritual through participation as it is that one lives in a fellowship where the gospel is experienced and thereby appropriated. When one interprets experience and formulates it as belief, one "learns" it. The substance of what is learned therefore depends on the qualities of life that are experienced. We have said that unless belief systems are validated, people cannot or do not remain committed to them, because they will gradually come to be viewed as not true. Miller's educational view is consistent. Love and forgiveness may become empty concepts unless they are experienced as realities in the community where the Spirit is present, the community which again and again "validates" the truth it professes.

What we have been saying is that the very nature of belief and belief systems necessitates the existence of some such agency as the church, including the family unit. Beliefs are "sustained, reformed, and embodied by the faith community," according to our thesis. Participation is therefore a presupposition for belief formation and a context for any teaching that relates to belief.

Lest we assume that the church is a kind of self-contained organization with its belief system and its structure, we should remind ourselves that the very content of the belief is formulated in the context of the broader "world," and that it calls for reaching out, for ministry to those outside the community. How does the church deal with the growing "invisible religion," which is a privatized, individually experienced affair, expressed in isolation?[7] If there were expressed beliefs in this religious phenomenon, it would be easier to deal with it, but such research as has been done, centering mostly around the theory of J. Milton Yinger, points toward the conclusion that the "invisible religion" is non-doctrinal, and certainly that it does not form a unitary belief system.[8] Where does this religion come from? Is it the result of the impact of mass media? Robert Lynn asks, "Will the churches be able to come to terms with a media-oriented society?" He adds:

> Other forces in American society have long recognized and feared the potential educational power exercised by the major television networks. Indeed both the political left and right can agree on one thing: The network moguls are, in effect, the value-brokers of contemporary America.[9]

Most people would have to give a negative response to Lynn's question, because we have failed to recognize that, as he says, "television constitutes our society's cultural mainstream and embodies a potent form of religion."[10]

Certainly the "electronic church" seems to increase the problem, rather than to alleviate it. To participate in a community of faith, seeking first of all to *understand* these cultural phenomena, and then to work out responsible ways of dealing with them, in the light of belief, would be to experience confirmations of those aspects of the Christian belief system that deal with transformation of culture. Moreover, participants would be taking a step toward developing a perspective for themselves which would help integrate the competing life worlds emerging in a pluralistic, secular culture. Since research indicates great need in "help for the individual in integrating the various fractionated aspects of his existence,"[11] then vigorous analysis of the belief system itself may need to take place within the church. Borhek and Curtis point out that as churches become another bureaucracy and the duties of ministry are broadened to take on more and more responsibilities, "many urbanites find that rather than integrating their lives, churches provide them with a new set of specialized roles and statuses which are more than ever walled off from the rest of their lives."[12] From the perspective of sociology of belief, the authors become almost prescriptive or exhortatory at this point. If churches produce further fragmentation, rather than help overcome it, the personal results may be drastic. It would be possible to take this concern and work on it; there are many implications for worship and preaching, for small group organization and life, maybe even for intentional communities. But that is not our task here. We have been engaging in a kind of critique of the community life in which Christians participate because of its possibility for confirming or negating beliefs as they are studied and formed. And of course that kind of critical reflection, carried on by participants in the community, may result in reformation of both life and belief.

Growth of the self

One frame of reference for belief development is the community of faith. Another is the person, and where that person "is" developmentally and situationally. After all, it is the individual, the self (the union of all the facets of a human being in a particular identity) who thinks, feels, acts, believes. Toulmin, already quoted, holds together the community and the self, the conceptual inheritance made available through enculturation, and the native capacity and role of the individual. That position is basic to anything that is said here about the individual. Even the rapidly developing neuro-sciences assume that "the fabric of the brain is set down as a result of the interaction of genetic blueprints and environmental influences."[13] Research indicates that the "genetic contribution," if not used, will disappear, but "is capable of further development given the optimal environmental stimulation." (Actual "marked changes

in brain development" are observable in rats reared in an enriched environment, in contrast to those reared in an impoverished environment.)[14] One
scientist refers to the "mysteries" of the brain and its "exquisitely built tis-
sue."[15] We can only share the sense of wonder as we think of the initiating and
responding power of the brain as a physical entity. There is interaction with the
environment, true, but there is also the "communication" between those parts
of the brain controlling motor behavior and those controlling emotions or
thought, for example. Thinking, feeling, and acting influence one another, and
no "domain" can be isolated. Material and spiritual cannot be separated. Hebrew anthropology is confirmed.

When we think about the development of belief, then, we must do our
thinking in the context of the unity of the self. We have already said that belief
has an affective as well as a cognitive aspect, and that it predisposes one to
action. One can give a clear cognitive explication of baptism, to return to an
earlier example, but unless one *cares,* feeling that it is important, that it enables
belonging and contributes to selfhood, it is not likely to be a significant belief.
Much work has been done by educators in the domains of learning—cognitive,
affective, and psychomotor.[16] Reference will be made to those later in consideration of models of teaching. Here the point is that all are important in the
growth of the self. Some educators have insisted that we have overemphasized
the cognitive aspects of faith, to the detriment of the affective. That may be
the case, so that some persons may never have known the deep sense of trust
and of cherishing that marks living faith. It may also be the case (probably
more likely *is* the case) that a person has never known the affective dimension
of excitement as an emotion accompanying some moment of cognitive insight
because the cognitive has never been taken seriously enough. Our task may well
be to think of ways to overcome what may have been meager beliefs and impoverished faith.

To see the growing self as a context to be considered for belief formation is
to be reminded of another key point: that the same type beliefs are neither
possible nor desirable for every age. Rokeach's primitive beliefs, built up in the
central region of the self out of early experiences of the child, in a pre-conceptual
period, are largely dependent on what happens in the family and the community
of which the child is a part. Later, to use Jean Piaget's categories, as the child
moves through the period of concrete operational thought, beginning at about
age six or seven, and then formal operational thought, beginning at about age
eleven or twelve, it is possible to see how data is processed, first as concrete facts,
then as concepts requiring formal or abstract reasoning powers. It is only in this
last stage that a person is capable of testing the adequacy of a belief system, its
inner logic and coherence, its integrative function, its reference potentiality for
moral action. Much work has been done by developmental theorists, including
implications for suitable educational approaches to various age groups. That will

have to be assumed here, and used where appropriate rather than re-presented or interpreted.[17] Theorists like Jean Piaget, Jerome Bruner, Lawrence Kohlberg, and James Fowler warn us about the dangers of putting people in categories, of judging stages by an adult norm.

John Westerhoff, who has made use of stage theories, heeds that warning in his own approach. His analogy of a tree and faith development is a good way to conclude our reflections on the growth of the self. Westerhoff speaks of styles of faith, rather than stages, although ordinarily these styles do develop in a particular sequence—experienced faith, affiliative faith, searching faith, owned faith. Faith development is like the expanding rings of a tree, he says. Even in its first year, a tree of one ring is still "a complete and whole tree." A tree does not eliminate rings, but expands and adds them, responding to environment, just as a person grows, interacting with "other faithing selves in a community of faith."[18] Here is where the native potential and the ordinary processes of growth move back again into the community context.

The shaping influence of action

Any dimension of the life of a person—interest, need, motive, activity— might be considered a context for belief. Any programmatic part of a congregation might be examined for its impact on belief. Because it is necessary to be selective, and because engagement in mission or in action is the avenue *par excellence* for several contemporary educators, it seems appropriate here to reflect on action as the context for development of belief. The saying "We are more likely to act our way into believing than to believe our way into acting" seems to be public property.[19] It is consistent with what the eleventh grader said in a discussion on belief and behavior, described in chapter 2, where she recognized the human tendency to rationalize behavior by constructing beliefs. It is consistent with the findings of psychologist David Myers, reported in *The Human Puzzle.* In one section, "Behavior and Belief," he reports on observations and research dealing with "the contribution of action to belief and attitudes." For example, he says that "people will believe in what they stand up for,"[20] and that roles people take in an organization, including the church, help shape what they believe and value. He talks about Benjamin Franklin, who requested a small personal favor from an opponent, and won a friend. He talks about reality therapy, where therapists attempt to shape or induce behavior as the entry to disposition and attitudes. It is clear to Myers, from his wide overview of research, that overt acts influence beliefs, attitudes, and disposition. It seems significant, to cite some recent history, that research reports show that since the 1954 Supreme Court school desegregation decision, "the percentage of white Americans favoring integrated schools has approximately doubled," and since the 1964 Civil Rights Act, conviction about willingness to have persons of other races as friends and neighbors has changed positively.[21] Myers is not advocating the view that there is a one-way relationship, moving from behavior as cause to belief as result. Usually, he says, educationally we have assumed the opposite point of view, that belief determines behavior. The time has come, he concludes, to recognize that "new understandings of social psychology affirm and enliven some ancient biblical truths."[22] The work of Myers is more informative and comprehensive than can be reported here. His focus on the importance of action, of the deed, is his approach to strengthening the New Testament view "of the bond between right action and true belief."[23]

What we have already said, with respect to the nature of belief, is that belief and action are interactive and interdependent. It becomes more important to remember that assumption as we ask how teaching influences belief.

The unifying function of purpose

One of the most devastating comments made by young people, as reported in *Five Cries of Youth,* is that adults do not know the purpose of the church.[24] For every group, every institution, every action, when there has been a clear sense of purpose, a consciousness of mission, then life, belief, attitudes all seem to cohere. Everything is held together and unified around purpose. In recent history, Cuba's literacy campaign is a dramatic example of that fact. Jonathan Kozol calls it the "untold education story of our generation."[25] His purpose is not to interpret nor advocate Castro's Marxism, but rather to determine how, within one year, more than one million illiterate Cubans could be taught to read and write. When Castro said in a speech to the United Nations in September 1960 that within a year, Cuba would become the first country of America able to say that it had not one illiterate person, the world almost disregarded his remarks. But Cuba believed him. More than 100,000 boys and girls, mostly between the ages of ten and fourteen, became student-volunteers. They were trained, sent to live in the homes of their "students," where they identified with them, worked with them and taught them. These thousands of young Cubans spent nearly a year "risking their lives, working like fanatics, living on little more than six hours of sleep in the same house and often in the same room as some of the poorest campesinos in the land."[26] In spite of problems, they succeeded. Loyalty to Castro may have been a beginning point. Ideological formulations followed, rather than preceded, this educational "Great Campaign of 1961." From all Kozol's research, including his interviews with participant teachers who "learned the greatest lessons of their lives," his impression is of "the total sense of ethical exhilaration of the literacy struggle."[27]

The same kind of thing happened in Nicaragua in the National Literacy Campaign that ended in August 1980. More than 400,000 Nicaraguans responded to the hard work of the young *brigadistas* ("student-volunteers"). They "learned to master basic reading and writing skills," at the same time that "tens of thousands of young people and their families learned about rural poverty and peasant culture."[28] What was evident here, as in Cuba, was a "commitment of the spirit," a sense of purpose, that prevailed against seemingly insurmountable odds.

One wonders why these stories have not been told more often and more widely. Whatever the reason, it brings before us a vivid picture of what can happen when people are caught up in a sense of mission. We cannot contrive such a situation, of course, but we can seek to be clearer about the "why" of our lives and our calling, and, from time to time, in small ways or even great ones, we may be blessed with a new sense of purpose.

In light of all that has been said here, one might conclude that belief formation is too complex a matter to do anything about, or that education, if it is to be directed toward belief formation, must control all the forces, the contexts, that impinge upon the person. Neither option is recommended. Rather, working in the kind of arena described here, teaching can still be done in such a way that it fulfills a unique function, consistent with the way belief systems develop, and even contributing, as Toulmin suggests, to the improvement of our "forms of life and understanding." Consider several observations about teaching.

Teaching

First of all, teaching presupposes but is not the same thing as the process of enculturation or socialization. Socialization is perhaps a better process to relate to faith development, and teaching to belief development, although they cannot be so neatly separated. It may be appropriate to say that learning takes place through socialization. It is inaccurate to say that teaching depends solely on or is to be carried out primarily through socialization, intentional or otherwise. And it only contributes to muddled categories to say that all experiences educate, or that experience is the best teacher.

Second, teaching within the context of the church is a form or function of ministry. Everything said about purpose, mission, action, suggests that to isolate teaching into a separate compartment is to undercut its effectiveness, at least when we are talking about belief formation. Protestants could learn much from the Roman Catholic view of catechesis, a pastoral activity, an ecclesial action, dealing with the responsibilities for leading persons to maturity of faith as they develop a "Christian interpretation to human events."[29] Their official *General Catechetical Directory* states it like this:

> Catechesis is concerned with the community, but it does not neglect the individual believer. It is linked with the other pastoral functions of the Church, but it does not lose its own specific character. At one and the same time it performs the functions of initiation, education, and formation.
>
> It is very important that catechesis retain the richness of these various aspects in such a way that one aspect is not separated from the rest to the detriment of the others.[30]

It is not difficult to see teaching as an integral part of catechesis. Both are forms of ministry.

Third, teaching is not to be equated with schooling. Schooling *does* deal with teaching and learning, but it is not the only setting in which these processes occur. To set schooling over against socialization or "intergenerational learning" or the affective domain is to confuse issues and to set up a straw object as a scapegoat. When one looks for opportunities for teaching in a church, and sees how a minister could use committee work or community issues to deal with matters of belief, it is somewhat preposterous to rely only on a school of the church.

Fourth, teaching deals with the development of understanding. That seems to be the function that distinguishes it from other activities, or other functions of ministry. Charles Melchert is one of the few educational theorists dealing seriously with the concept of understanding. For him, understanding is "a cognitive process of structuring experience or data."[31] But persons, depending on their varying styles of learning and expressing, may differ in the ways they structure and thereby "understand" experience. Some persons, for example, Melchert says, may best come to understand through dance or acrobatics.[32] His approach is suggestive for the understanding of teaching assumed here, a concept to be developed more fully in the next chapters.

Fifth, the person of the teacher makes a difference. Some rather amazing research confirms the possibility of influences of a teacher. Contradicting much other research about the influence of schooling on adult status, one group of researchers stumbled on some information which, when explored, showed that one first grade teacher, over a period of years, had a remarkable influence extending through the adult status of sixty children she taught. Everyone remembered her. She did her work "with a lot of love," confidence in children, and extra help for those who needed it, so that everyone always learned to read. She left first graders with a "profound impression of the importance of schooling,"[33] and with a solid base for later learning.

To point to this kind of teacher or to say that a teacher is important may be to place a load of guilt on the conscientious teacher who seeks to produce observable results or to clarify beliefs or "make" better Christians out of students during a given class period. That is not the intention. Rather, it is to say that the teacher who cares—and that is probably most important of all—and who knows how to learn may be of benefit to others. Aquinas, dealing with Augustine's statement that only God is Teacher, says that Augustine "does not intend to exclude man from teaching exteriorly, but intends to say that God alone teaches interiorly." The "true teacher" does not endow the mind with light, but supplies "external help to it to reach the perfection of knowledge."[34] Aquinas distinguishes between learning by "discovery" and learning by "instruction," and encourages the teacher to lead "the pupil to knowledge of things he does not know in the same way that one directs himself through the process of discovering something he does not know."[35] The teacher who has this kind of ability to learn and to teach, combined with a dependence on God, finds a resulting freedom to work with recognition of limitations and courage to risk failure or to refuse control over others. Such a one may indeed be a rare person, but the vision of that person offers a direction for growth.

What, then, shall be our approach to teaching?

4

INTENTIONALITY and TEACHING

Four assumptions, to be explored in order, underlie the work to be done on teaching in the remainder of this book—

> *that the existing situation calls for more direct, conscious attention to belief formation as an emphasis of the teaching ministry of the church;*

> *that to be a teacher is to be intentional;*

> *that familiarity with domains and levels of knowledge is an aid to being intentional;*

> *that understanding and being able to use models or approaches with clear purposes and strategies give a basis for choice, and therefore for drawing on appropriate knowledge and skills to develop teaching activities congruent with one's vision of what he/she is about.*

Polls and practices

According to the report of the Princeton Religion Research Center, although 55% of Americans say they find religion "very important," this 1980 figure is a decline from the 75% holding such a view in 1952.[1] Even more startling is a trend with respect to religious training. Over the last quarter of the century, persons who received religious training as a child declined from 94% in 1952 to 83% in 1978, and for those who wanted their children to receive religious instruction, there was a decline from 98% in 1952 to 87% in 1978.[2] One might raise what could turn out to be a kind of "chicken-and-egg" question: Has the decline of interest in religious instruction produced a decline in concern about religion? There are other hypotheses one might project—for example, that religious instruction, or even perhaps life within the church, has not been effective. However, polls, which point to statistical evidence of existing conditions, do not explicate causes of those conditions. There is some comfort in the fact that there is more evidence of the value placed on religion in 1980 than in 1978, and that there is a kind of leveling off of the general long decline in church membership, attendance, and interest in things religious.[3] There is also evidence, in the 1980 Princeton report, which focused more on belief, that 94% of U.S. Americans say they believe in a supreme deity, and that for 57%, religious *beliefs* are very important; for 27%, fairly important.[4] For young people, 95% say they believe in God. For 42%, belief is very important; for 43%, fairly important.[5] Note that there is a difference between youth and adults. In spite of the seemingly religious orientation, teenagers are "to a considerable extent 'turned off' by churches and organized religion."[6] When effort has been made to determine something of the content of belief, 41% of youth hold what is called "authoritative belief,"[7] dependent more on external authority than on understanding. (Westerhoff would call this "affiliative" faith.)

In reflecting on his polls, Gallup says he has "an uneasy feeling," and that "the 1980's may be a decade of discontent," or even may be marked by "a moral crisis of the first dimension."[8] Even with such evidence of *attested* beliefs, it is to be questioned whether there is always significant relationship between belief and meaning in life, or belief and responsible behavior. Yet Merton Strommen, on the basis of his research which does try to explore such relationships, contends that "there is nothing as powerful in predicting a Lutheran's attitudes or his behavior as knowing what he values and believes."[9] In any case, statistical evidence points not to complacency but to confirmation of our beginning assumption that the present situation calls for attention to belief, to a particular kind of belief—"enabling belief" that grows out of the living faith of a community, and gives meaning and direction to life. What we have done, essentially, then, is to review and reaffirm some of the early explorations, including the major thesis of this study.

Why teachers teach

Do teachers teach subjects or people? Is religion caught or taught? These clichés pose false dilemmas. Like the over-simplistic contrasting of traditional and experiential education as the equivalent of bad and good or old and new, they blur the intelligent and deliberate decisions that teachers must make in what is a complex matter. If, instead, we could say that teachers teach in order to help persons understand, so that they could determine the meaning of a subject for themselves, we would be on safe territory. There would be an obligation for teachers always to be in the process of trying to understand for themselves, to be careful about responsibility for the integrity of a subject and for truth, as well as for the needs of a student. Respecting, caring for, nurturing the will to learn in the student would call for a teacher's effort to help persons understand enough for themselves so that they could decide what the meaning for them would be. And there would be the support of those learners in their efforts to assimilate that meaning for themselves. A teacher therefore would never *impose* his or her own beliefs, although it would be appropriate on occasions to offer a belief, and certainly to participate with others in working together to interpret belief systems of the community.

Thomas Green, already quoted with reference to core beliefs, holds the view that to teach is to help people be able to answer the question "why?" That is, it has to do with the *grounds* for belief as well as with the *content* of belief. It has to do with the use of intelligence, and for both teacher and student, with the pursuit of truth. Because some activities that often pass for teaching—conditioning, training, indoctrinating—do not focus on "why?" or on thinking, they are not at the heart of teaching, for Green, although in certain situations they may appropriately be used as teaching activities. He uses the term "instructing" as being nearest to genuine teaching. Some other term might have been more suggestive of his position, but as he uses it, it is clear that "instructing" has to do with the development of "enabling beliefs," those that overcome fragmentation and give direction to life. All of this has to do with teaching that is directed toward the development of a person who sees "life as a whole."[10] Obviously, Green is concerned with *how* persons believe as well as with *what* they believe. Hence his attitude of desiring both openness and conviction, for teacher as well as for student. It is an attitude characterized by curiosity, rooted in wonder, as with Plato and Hannah Arendt. When that is the case, "then reflection and study become not tasks, but necessities—as spontaneous and essential for life as breathing."[11]

Green and others like him know *why* they teach. To explore this idea of teaching is to move toward a proposal—that to be a teacher is to be intentional. Robert Menges says it clearly.

> Intentionality is the dimension underlying my conception of teaching. The intentional teacher is one whose actions and intentions are congruent. Such teachers know what they intend and are able to select appropriate means for themselves and for their students to actualize those intentions.[12]

He goes on to say that this view holds teaching to be an art, but "does not ignore the particular skills of teaching." It opens up a wide variety of roles to the teacher. And it "emphasizes personal and uniquely human qualities of the teacher and the learner as well as characteristics of the subject matter."[13]

Menges explores the concept of intentionality which he sees as underlying particular intentions. Intentionality is a way of uniting thought, will, and action. It is an intriguing concept, with implications for all human existence. Moreover, it is related to what has been said about belief systems, in that intentionality moves belief from an unconscious to a conscious level. But that concept cannot be pursued here.

With respect to teaching, intentionality brings a long-range view or purpose —perhaps hope is the better term—which enables a teacher to plan and act with a sense of clarity and direction. One component in that intentionality, in the approach suggested here, is the desire to work on belief formation, to help people be more thoughtful and more able to know and say what they believe and why.

Such an emphasis seems especially needed at this particular moment in history.

A warning is in order. To force four-year-olds to verbalize belief in salvation or to turn every lesson or sermon or retreat into a discussion or lecture on belief would be more than an absurdity. It would be a fatal blow to the possibility of developing beliefs that would be "indicators" or "springs" or powers capable of generating meaning and guiding people, as James Dittes says. In order to aid in the development of belief, one should not concentrate all the time directly on belief. On the other hand, a kind of general awareness will enable a teacher to utilize informal occasions as well as to plan for teaching efforts that will deliberately deal with belief in appropriate ways.

To move from a generalized intentionality to specific intentions is to take a major step in deciding what and how to teach. If one's *intention* is to transmit facts or explicate concepts, then lectures, programmed instruction, reading, and testing are possibilities. A report on Calvin's view or a word study of the biblical treatment of certain ideas should have come earlier in the process. There are numerous possible intentions. Obviously, one cannot do everything at once, but to begin with intentions is to have an organizing focus and a basis for planning and setting up a sequence of learning activities. The third and fourth assumptions listed at the beginning of this chapter, relating to domains and levels of knowledge, and to models of teaching, have to do with ways of taking hold of the intention and moving toward implementing it in teaching.

Domains and levels of knowledge

Most frequent reference to the spheres or territories of human learning within which knowledge is developed is to the cognitive, affective, and psychomotor domains. Possibly this is because of the work that has been done by educators on objectives for these domains. In addition, particularly among religious educators, reference is often made to volitional elements, having to do with the will, and sometimes to the conative, having to do with desire, will, or drives impelling toward action. Although recognizing that there are other forces within the individual that influence learning—the physiological or the existential, for example—we will refer here only to the cognitive and affective domains, drawing on the available taxonomies. For the psychomotor domain, taxonomies refer primarily to reflex actions and physical movement patterns rather than to the kind of behavior contributing more directly to belief formation. In any case, reference to domains and levels of knowledge is only suggestive of one way of moving beyond recognized intention to actual teaching.

Benjamin Bloom and his associates propose that the intellectual, rational powers of the individual, operative primarily through the cognitive domain, function through six levels:

Knowledge	Application	Synthesis
Comprehension	Analysis	Evaluation[14]

With the exception of the first two, the meaning of the categories seems self-evident. For those two, the lowest levels of the cognitive domain, other terms would have been preferable. Norris Sanders, in planning how to devise questions that would lead to each level, renames "knowledge" as "memory," and "comprehension" is divided into "translation" and "interpretation."[15] The lowest level has to do with facts, with recall or memory. Comprehension has to do with translating information into other terms, not just remembering it, and with relating or interpreting it, as Sanders points out. What is important is for a teacher to be aware of the level at which work is being done. There is a vast difference between "Who is John the Baptist?" (memory) and "Identify the major themes of Reformed theology" (analysis) and "What is your judgment about the three views of human nature you have studied?" (evaluation). The levels are cumulative; each one is incorporated into and necessary for the next level. It is inappropriate to evaluate Calvin's view of sin without being able to state it, analyze it, compare it. But it is also inappropriate—the better word is wrong—to spend a lifetime of recalling facts, never doing anything with them, reacting to them, forming one's own position about them.

To build belief systems, every level of knowledge is important and has a place. In a sense, one has to earn the right to evaluate, so that a teacher should be alert to levels in relation to ages and readiness for evaluating a position. When a person moves to the level of synthesis and evaluation, there is the possibility of dealing with core beliefs, clusters of beliefs, and their relations—relations viewed both psychologically and logically. All of this means that a teacher may have to find ways of assessing where a person is, in order not to move over the same territory endlessly. The excitement of learning—of acquiring new information, of manipulating facts or ideas to place them in new categories, of rearranging information to fit new tasks, of reviewing knowledge to see whether it has been comprehended and "used" properly[16]—has within it an affective dimension that becomes motivational.

The affective domain is also one that is more than a climate or a support that aids satisfactory cognitive functioning. It is that, of course, but it is also a domain to be approached directly on occasions. Persons concerned with values often refer to three levels—facts, concepts, values. The assumption is that to stop short of becoming aware of one's values and of being committed to them is in essence not to be able to take responsibility for them and for one's actions. These are the levels listed by David Krathwohl and associates:

Receiving
Responding
Valuing
Organization
Characterization by a value or value complex[17]

Notice that the first three of these have to do with feeling, with emotional response. One may simply receive information with no real reaction, or at the next level may respond in some way—with delight, with disgust. Valuing has to do with preferring, with cherishing. The next level moves into the cognitive domain also, as a dimension of commitment to a particular conceptualization. Finally, in the deepest level, there is also involvement of volition and behavioral factors as a person develops a lifestyle expressive of that which is cared about and understood.

The levels chosen are suggestive of the fact that domains can never be completely separated; only temporarily so. If a person never is aware of feeling, never encouraged to say or respond through artistic form or committed affirmation in words to belief or self-awareness or others, it is not likely that the lifestyle can be expressive of the person's being. But to force expression too soon, as without adequate knowledge, or too often, is to be aware of the domains of human learning, but not of levels.

How do domains and levels relate to intentional teaching? Consider a specific situation, an eleventh grade unit of church school work on the life of Christ. A teacher, knowing that the group has had extensive work at the lower cognitive levels of memory, interpretation, and analysis, decides to focus particularly on the level of synthesis. In the affective domain, the focus is to be on the valuing level. After concise, rapidly moving reviews of names, time-lines, and favorite stories, with opportunities to respond to how one felt about illustrative persons and events, the class moves into the main portion of work—reading novels on the life of Christ and discussing them, offering their personal judgments about the validity of the portrayal. As preparation for the last session, to be held as a weekend retreat, each young person brings a one-page description of three or four persons from literature whose lives have been significantly shaped by Jesus Christ. At the retreat, the youth role-play the characters, setting up imaginary conversations in which they portray the impact of the Lord. Perhaps—just perhaps—the situation may develop in such a way that persons may start to speak of their own experience, and thus assimilate, or internalize, meaning. The response of the teacher at this point comes out of his/her artistic, aesthetic intuition. In any case, there is the possibility during these last few sessions at the retreat for affective and cognitive elements to come together, probably in worship.

There are many other possibilities for procedure. The important thing is that the teacher know what is intended. Then, in the act of teaching, it is possible to pull together, to unify all that is known about subject matter, developmental stages, domains, levels, and the situation of particular individuals.

One other ingredient is helpful at that planning point—to have a set of options upon which to draw, suggestive of alternative directions, purposes, and procedures, options which hold together theory and practice.

Approaches and models

During recent years, when the term "model" has become current in many fields, educators have come to value the contribution of the concept to teaching.

According to Bruce Joyce and Marsha Weil, whose influential *Models of Teaching* is an aid to teachers in making intentional decisions, a model "is a plan or pattern that can be used to shape curriculums (long-term courses of studies), to design instructional materials, and to guide instruction in the classroom and other settings."[18] It is a blueprint or representation or paradigm that serves as a guide for organization of subject matter, choice of strategies or methods, and determination of teacher role, but most of all, it helps a teacher to answer a question: What "mission" is to be accomplished in this teaching, and what are the appropriate forms and procedures through which that mission can be accomplished?

Many of the models presented by Joyce and Weil are useful in church education. They group the models in four categories: information-processing, social, personal, and behavioral. Here, more attention is of necessity given to approaches or families than to specific models, using, but adapting and adding to the Joyce and Weil groupings to form five clusters of approaches: information-processing, group interaction, indirect communication, personal development, and action/reflection. The mission is suggested in the focus. The relating of the approach to belief formation is a way of beginning a reflection process with teachers concerned to develop through teaching some of the ideas being considered. The following chapters, then, should give even more specific help, so that teaching can become a kind of activity directed toward helping persons develop "owned" beliefs.

The chart offered here (pp. 40–41) gives a comparative overview of the five approaches selected. Several general comments are in order. All these approaches are possibilities for all age levels, when appropriately used or adapted. The information-processing that an adult would use would be different from that of the fifth grader; comparing doctrinal themes of Luther and Wesley would be different from listing and identifying Jesus' apostles. The indirect communication that a teacher would use in a story told to three-year-olds and in a film based on Plato's parable of the cave would be quite different.

All these approaches and models still require planning with attention to organization of subject matter, objectives, methods. The difference now is that one has a major advantage in making a decision as to where to start. In choosing an approach where the general purpose or mission is known, it is possible to move quickly from subject matter and people to approach. All the skills of teaching are resources. That is the case about methods. But now—and this is the most important part of all—one does not draw just on a new method or an interesting activity or the latest fad. One can utilize those strategies which most directly move toward accomplishment of the intention, toward giving appropriate forms to theory.

Finally, a models approach to teaching stands as an alternative to the effort to find and use the "best" way to teach.[19] A person can and should have what is called a "bread-and-butter model," one providing a kind of security and competence, a base of operation. But to be a "real" teacher is to be able to choose from among options that one which is best for particular purposes in relation to particular subjects and persons. It is to be able to use models in sequences or combinations. With respect to belief, then, it becomes possible to deal intentionally with levels and types of belief, viewed as a part of the overall content of teaching.

These general comments should be remembered as the next five chapters are developed. Rationale is expanded; specific suggestions for implementation are included. To know what is available is a key component in becoming an "intentional teacher." Although there may be other approaches than the ones described here, and certainly there are dozens more models than the few referred to, what is offered suggests a basic frame of reference for thinking about teaching, as well as a way of focusing teaching on belief formation. Each approach or family of models is developed in terms of its basic characteristics, several specific illustrations, and concluding reflections.

	INFORMATION-PROCESSING	GROUP INTERACTION
Focus	Understanding, primarily through the process of thinking.	Building knowledge and social responsibility through participating in group interaction.
Rationale	Human beings need ways to handle facts, to impose a structure on knowledge, to interpret experience, to develop "conceptual goggles" which can be used to make sense out of life.	Because people learn from one another and together construct knowledge in an interactive process where content is both conceptual and relational or non-verbal, the group influences the "becoming" self as well as the development of belief.
Description	All types of thinking activities—recalling, grouping, naming, analyzing, interpreting, etc., are ways of acquiring information, storing it so that it can be retrieved and related. Inquiry into a problem may do this, or hearing a lecture may do it. Important: this approach is characterized by interaction between the general and the particular, so that propositions or concepts can always be documented by concrete data.	Clarifying and interpreting ideas, testing them against the perception of others and against understanding of tradition or application to the present, the group seeks answers to questions, does research and reports, discusses, evaluates both conclusions and learning process.
Contribution to belief formation	The Christian's inheritance—persons, events, their interpretations, creeds—can be known and processed through the kinds of thinking activities emphasized here, so that a common memory and language can be developed. But this knowledge must be related to ongoing experience so persons "use" it, through other activities of thinking which lead to understanding. This is the most direct approach to "faith's asking the intellect for help."	Because the community of faith is the context for belief, it has potential for becoming a fellowship where there is a mutuality of support as persons relate belief to faith in a frame of reference that links past and present in the search for meaning.

INDIRECT COMMUNICATION	PERSONAL DEVELOPMENT	ACTION/ REFLECTION
Self-examination and encounter with the truth.	Development of the powers of the self through awareness and expression.	"Doing" the truth, with thinking which informs and evaluates action.
Art has a potential for communicating that crosses boundaries, that involves the whole person at various levels of identification and confrontation. Or in artistic expression, there is the possibility of experiencing meaning in a way that changes both self and others.	When a person becomes aware of self and environment, feeling accepted and able to function as a contributing individual, the powers of the self are engaged in a "becoming" that realizes the powers resident within the human being.	Often a person does not understand the meaning of an idea until it is expressed through action, and experience, reflected upon, is interpreted. "Praxis," an interactive relation of theory and practice, is a means of enabling relationship among the cognitive, volitional, and conative dimensions of the self.
Stories, parables, music, film, mass media open the door to involvement of responding, thinking, feeling persons, not as in art criticism, but through engagement and response.	Ways of helping people develop the sense of self are available; learning how to express ideas and feelings in imaginative ways; self-initiated, directed learning; sharing of perceptions; developing interpersonal skills.	Analysis of situations, drawing on both tradition and contemporary disciplines, problem-solving, testing and revising assumptions, are processes which bring action into relation with thought.
Believing has to do with a kind of understanding that includes but goes beyond the rational dimension. As persons move indirectly toward and into a kind of embodied truth, they are confronted by it, and in the experience of the "truth for me," they may appreciate it.	When a person is aware of being a unique self, loved and called into purpose, he/she is able to think more clearly and honestly, to "own" belief with increasing freedom, depth, and commitment.	The "word" of belief is informed and confirmed by the "deed" of obedience. Faithfulness is related to believing when experience, reflected on, is formulated as belief. Thus one acts one's way into believing.

BELIEVING
and THINKING
The Information-Processing Approach

Introduction

If this approach offers the most direct response to "faith's asking the intellect for help," as suggested in the overview chart of the preceding chapter (that chart is presupposed for this chapter and the next four), then it should be advantageous to consider some of the ways teachers go about helping persons "process information." How can persons acquire names and facts, store and organize them, relate them as concepts, interrelate concepts and experiences as beliefs? Another way to think about these processes is to use the computer programming language of input, manipulating data, and output. In fact, the information-processing terminology comes largely from the influence of efforts of computer scientists to utilize the normal workings of the human mind as models for setting up computer programs. In turn, modern cognitive psychologists use computer technology, along with other sources, as a stimulus to understand cognitive functioning.[1]

Other influences lie behind this approach, of course, all the way back to the Socratic dialogue and the lecture. John Dewey's *How We Think* offers a pattern which continues to be used by many persons in their problem-solving activities of thinking. Parallel to the great strides in computer programming between 1955–1960[2] are the strides in curriculum development related to cognitive learning theory. Jerome Bruner's *The Process of Education,* 1960, growing out of the Woods Hole Conference in 1959, is another major influence. Bruner has been influential in church education as well as in general curriculum development with his inquiry learning. Although dominant emphases as we move into the 1980s lean more toward confluent education, the information-processing cluster of approaches to teaching continues to be essential.

Characteristics

The three categories chosen for use in specifying some of the distinguishing marks of this first approach to teaching can be used to compare it with the other four approaches. In every case, comments are suggestions only. It quickly becomes apparent in the section on *Illustrations* that variations occur.

ROLE OF THE TEACHER:
controller—
of the subject matter and the way it is organized, when the teacher becomes
presenter
of the process set up to guide students' thinking in a planned sequence of
activities, when the teacher becomes director

ROLE OF THE LEARNER:
responder—
to material as presented
to concepts and insights emerging out of the process as specified

STRATEGIES:
development of intellectual freedom through helping persons learn how to
think, by—
stimulating thought processes through posing questions
organizing subject matter either logically or psychologically, so that it can
be presented clearly or investigated without waste of energy
organizing processes for investigating in a clear sequence of steps to be taken
by students, using inductive or deductive strategies as appropriate

Several additional general comments may help describe this approach. First,
along with the interest in content, there is an interest in helping students learn
how to think, and to develop their *own* system(s) for processing information.
There are different cognitive learning styles, and it helps a student, as well as a
teacher, to be aware of what is most effective for him or her, and what other
options are available. When persons know what is their characteristic way to
approach a task or a subject, they can improve it, or develop other ways. It is often
possible to build in discussions on the "how" of learning in most models. Even
when a lecture is presented, it is sometimes helpful to spend time conferring with
students about ways in which the subject was "processed" by the speaker.

Second, the concept of *structure* is one of the keys to this approach. People
bombarded with an endless array of unrelated facts cannot often remember or
use them. When a structure—preferably one's own—is imposed upon information or interpreted experience, storage, retrieval, and expansion or utilization of
information is possible. The relationship to ways of handling biblical, historical,
and theological facts and concepts, in the church's teaching, seems obvious.

Third, information processing can and should be directed toward various
levels of knowledge, taking into account the cognitive capacity of the learner.
The curious mind of the fourth grader can get acquainted with biblical persons
through stories, recalled in conversations and response to music or pictures.
The questioning mind of the tenth grader can analyze the qualities of King
David and the events of his reign to determine the qualities of a good king and

leader; activities take place on the analytic level. Often the mature mind is not challenged beyond the memory or recall level, and does not have the opportunity to seek meaning. Of course, there are times when a person capable of functioning at the level of synthesis and evaluation does not know the basic facts, and a kind of remedial work is necessary. In any case, ability to use concepts of developmental theory and levels of knowledge aids the intentional teacher.

Fourth, the teacher's "at-homeness" in the subject matter is crucial. In a way, of course, this is true for all teaching, but it is especially the case here. A person's own understanding of the subject matter is the key to the possibility of communicating, and of freedom to allow others to explore. And the *way* the teacher thinks, the attitude taken toward a subject, of continuing to learn, is important for the emphasis on the "how" of thinking.

Illustrations

When a biblical scholar leads a group of seminarians through the steps of the process she or he takes to investigate and understand a scripture passage, an information-processing approach to teaching is being used. The scholarly discipline of Old Testament or New Testament studies is the model that guides the teaching, just as it guides the independent work of the scholar-teacher. When a minister prepares for a sermon with an exegesis of a particular scripture passage, an information-processing model is in operation. There are many such models, guiding either individual thinking processes or teaching practices. Several of the ideas here are drawn from Bruce Joyce and Marsha Weil's *Models of Teaching*, in the information-processing section. Other ideas are available there. Most are easily adaptable to Christian education. What is to be done here is to suggest some activities indicative of what could go on in different models, without developing the models themselves.

1. How we think. John Dewey has already been cited as a person influential in the approach to teaching under consideration. For him, the intellectual aim of education is *"the formation of careful, alert, and thorough habits of thinking."*[3] His concern is not with the collection of data, but with reflective thought. He says this:

> Active, persistent, and careful consideration of any belief or supposed form of knowledge in the light of the grounds that support it, and the further conclusions to which it tends, constitutes reflective thought.[4]

Belief, where there are grounds for belief (and this points to the *use* of the data) has to do with understanding, or grasping the meaning, and that is "the central function of all reflection."[5] The five steps in reflective thought proposed by Dewey are these:

. . . the occurrence of a problem or a puzzling phenomenon; then observation, inspection of facts, to locate and clear up the problem; then the formation of a hypothesis or the suggestion of a possible solution together with its elaboration by reasoning; then the testing of the elaborated idea by using it as a guide to new observations and experimentations.[6]

Do these steps "fit" thinking related to Christian belief? Dewey's concern was not religious. He was influenced by scientific methodology, in a world coming to value science highly, but in spite of that fact, his concern was more with reflective thought than with scientific conclusions. It is his contention that the procedure he described, initiating curiosity and questioning, can guide effective thought, and be directed toward the seeking of significance and meaning. Note how many levels of knowledge are involved. Dewey's emphasis is on analysis and synthesis, on the need for both inductive and deductive strategies of reasoning, flowing into and out of one another, thus relating the particular and the general.

Assume that after a lengthy youth discussion on love, someone makes this statement: "The term *love* can no longer have significance for Christians. The corruption of the idea of love by mass media has made it useless as a central, unique quality of Christian existence." One young person, going home with confusion in her mind, decides to find out for herself what Christian love means. In consultation with the pastor, who suggests resources, she starts to work. She is her own "teacher-controller." Would Dewey's "steps" help? It seems so. An individual or a group, following the procedure, should end up with the necessary "grounds" for making a decision or stating a belief.

2. Advance organizer. Take the same situation and the same question, the meaning of the Christian concept of love. Suppose the pastor, instead of suggesting resources and serving as resource person when needed, is asked by the young people to come in and explain the term. One possible way to do this would be to use David Ausubel's model. It centers around the use of an advance organizer, a concise presentation of the essence of what is to be considered, a kind of "intellectual scaffolding" on which students could hang ideas, relate them, use them. It is more a substantive summary than a journalist's lead sentence, or an outline preview, although it serves as reference which can give unity to an entire presentation. Linkage to the students' present experience or knowledge, either before or after the presentation of the organizer, is important. What would follow would be the clearest possible unfolding of the organizer, with the use of diagrams or other visual aids, illustrations, images. Perhaps there would be assigned reading to answer specific questions, questions to test one's understanding, applications, and conclusions. Directed student activities may be interspersed with the presentations. What happens must be organized in such a way that the new knowledge is relevant to older knowledge, that each part of the presentation is an integral part of what precedes and follows, so that learning can be assimilated. The advance organizer, and subsumer organizers, serve as "cognitive bridges," and facilitate what Ausubel calls "meaningful learning."[7]

The first thing that comes to mind is probably a lecture. Ausubel sees that, or other forms of organization and presentation or investigation of subject matter, as a form of teaching that calls for no apology. Related to "reception learning," it is directed toward active, not passive, thought on the part of the student, whose task becomes a mental interaction with and internalization of ideas. The teacher first processes information, and then plans ways to present it. Designed "to strengthen students' *cognitive structures*,"[8] the model is a time and energy saver for students. No steps are possible here, because they depend on the teacher's understanding and ability to organize and interpret, thus engaging the critical thinking of students through the process.

In his *A Theory of Education*, Joseph Novak presents a position based largely on Ausubel's theory, and suggests that his empirical research confirms this theory. Perhaps if all lecturers met the qualifications proposed by Ausubel and Novak, the results would be positive. Certainly if the pastor with whom we began understood the concept of Christian love, needed information could be brought to the group and presented in a fashion that would enable them, too, to understand.

3. Inductive model. A quite different approach to teaching is to be found in Hilda Taba's inductive model, a teacher-guided pupil processing of information. Note that reference here is to a *model* of teaching, rather than to the inductive *strategy*, which can be a part of many models. The model moves through three phases: (1) concept formation, with listing of separate items, grouping into categories, and labeling; (2) interpretation, with inferring and generalizing from data; and (3) application, with hypotheses, exploration, and verification.[9]

An exercise from a church school teacher education guide by Doris Hill illustrates the first phase.

Samaria	lame man	Pharisee
Saul	Jerusalem	temple
Peter	Damascus	justification
miracle	Levite	Jericho
mercy	John	persecution
apostle	love	priest
inn	alms	conversion[10]
lawyer	disciple	

Obviously, as Doris Hill points out, there are several ways to group the terms, all the way from common nouns and proper nouns to the three Bible stories from which the terms were drawn—the Good Samaritan, the conversion of Paul, and the healing of the lame man.[11] "Eliciting questions" by the teacher are a key part of this model. What belongs together? Why? What do you call the category? If this beginning were to be followed by study of one or more of the Bible stories, through other phases, questions would again be crucial in helping students to interpret and apply what they read and talk about.

More complex subjects can be approached in the same way. A group lists themes from hymns, novels, pictures, Bible passages, or other sources, groups them, and labels them with appropriate titles. There is a move back into the sources to study, interpret, and apply the concepts.

There is a difference between concept formation and concept attainment. In concept formation, unorganized data is processed by students who move toward whatever concept emerges from their handling of the information. In Jerome Bruner's concept attainment model, teachers devise games, questions, guided activities, carefully sequenced to move toward "discovery" of the concept predetermined by the teacher. Other information-processing models move into other ways of building cognitive knowledge and improving the thinking power of the individual.

4 Programmed instruction. One way to acquire the "basic facts" or terminology of an area of study is through programmed materials, a closely sequenced set of student activities with immediate feedback on the correctness of response. Repetition and use of terms in a variety of settings are important. Joyce and Weil, in *Models of Teaching,* include programmed instruction in the behavioral family or cluster of models, rather than the information-processing group. That is a valid classification because, consistent with the operant conditioning learning theory on which it is based, programmed instruction is directed more toward *acquiring* information than *processing* it. Nonetheless, if facts are basic building blocks, it seems appropriate to include here a model directed toward memory, one level of knowledge, and to some degree toward comprehension. Both levels are basic to the possibility of information processing. Other programmed materials may be directed toward different aspects of learning, but the illustration here is chosen because of the great concern in the church with respect to what is often called biblical illiteracy. That is a valid, immediate kind of concern. But the focus here is on information as "building blocks" for belief formation, and believing.

Mastering Old Testament Facts, Volume 1, is part of a series by Madeline Beck and Lamar Williamson, an adaptation of programmed instruction to help an individual "learn the content and structure of the Old Testament in the shortest possible time."[12] The basic content has to do only with "outline and sequence, persons, places, events, and characteristic features."[13] All activities, pre-tests, and guided reading are answers to questions; post-tests have to do with memory.

Look at the three questions from the introductory unit, included as checks after the pre-test, followed by guided reading and study of illustrations.

1. When applied to the Bible, the word "canon" means:
   a. A large gun used by field artillery units in the army.
   b. A list of writings accepted as Sacred Scripture.
   c. An ordained churchman connected with a cathedral.
   d. A body of church law.
2. The original meaning of canon, "measuring rod," referred to:
   a. The length of the list of books in the Bible.
   b. The church official who enforced the authority of the Bible.
   c. The religious body which resolved debates about the Scripture.
   d. The standards used in deciding which books to include in the Bible.

Fill in the blanks:

3. The three main forms of the Old Testament canon are _____,
   _____, and _____.
4. The two main differences among these three canons are (a) which _____
   are included and (b) how they are _____.[14]

Groups can go beyond the individual study and meet together to discuss the questions or interpretations of the content. But achievement of the stated goal of 90% mastery of the material would provide a working vocabulary for students, according to the authors. They warn that the emphasis on knowledge of content leaves out the vast history, intricate literary forms, matters of faith and ethics. What is offered are "indispensable building materials" for those seriously interested in building life "upon the God of the Bible in the community of faith which gave birth to the Bible and still lives from it."[15]

Reflections

Continuing to use the analogy of building, Beck and Williamson go on to say it is their wish that "on this trip to the lumber yard you will meet the Architect who can be found there and seize the opportunity to inquire how best to get on with your building."[16] Whether it is in congregational or graduate-level teaching, no doubt that statement would express the hope of many teachers intentionally choosing the information-processing models of teaching, using them to accomplish the purposes intrinsic to the approach.

Moving again to concern for belief formation, we get a picture of teaching which has to do with building, with forming. Often this approach requires the use of restraint on the part of the teacher, in order not to jump prematurely to force belief. That would be to equate memory with belief, or to confuse indoctrination with teaching—teaching concerned with the "why" or grounds for belief. And there is use of disciplined planning by the teacher who knows that what is done in a given teaching situation is only part of a long process.

There are several other observations that can be made now about the relation of this approach to development of belief. Characteristics and illustrations of the approach offer concrete content for earlier generalizations. Further, it should be apparent that no analysis of an approach to teaching can get at the unconscious levels of knowledge or hope of the teacher. For example, work on computer-based programs of information processing draws on statements of experts as to how they approach a task. It quickly becomes apparent that it is impossible to verbalize all that the "experts" know. They work from a tacit knowledge that goes beyond a computer. Similarly, with respect to the functioning of a teacher, there is the availability of a kind of tacit knowledge which is used intuitively and appropriately to bring a degree of life to information processing, one that cannot be captured in description or analysis. More important, there is the teacher's unconscious level of hope that students will "meet the Architect," and it is that hope which provides motivation for the disciplined efforts of the teacher, as well as a pervasive spirit of care, adding to the cognitive values of this model a nurturant climate.

It should also be said that whatever information or content is processed has within it the potential for *changing the person*. How this happens is a mystery as yet unraveled by human efforts. When a person starts to investigate some idea —Christian love, in the case of the young person and group mentioned here— there is both a risk and a potential of being changed by what is discovered. When Meno asked Socrates whether virtue could be taught, there began a maieutic process in which Socrates helped Meno use reason to its fullest in beginning to understand virtue. (Thus the Socratic "method" is another form of information processing.) Was the goal achieved or the question answered? That question remains unanswered. What is to be observed is that Socrates infected Meno with "the perplexity I feel myself,"[17] and in the process in which Meno became involved, something happened to him. The imperious, wealthy young aristocrat seemed somehow to become less assured, quieter, perhaps more virtuous.

Emphasis on content, especially characteristic of the Reformed tradition, has behind it the assumption that in the thinking, understanding process of engagement with content, something happens to the person. Thus the stress on biblical and theological subject matter, and the concern with *what* is taught and learned. Calvin's doctrine has transformational power. (See Chapter 2, p. 20.) Knowledge is not a matter of pride, and belief does more than bring integration to life. Thought is valued, not just for itself—even non-Calvinists like Dewey take "delight in thinking for the sake of thinking"[18]—but because it is a service of the mind, the response of the grateful person who wishes faith to be informed by understanding. As Marc Belth says, "even love, unformed by thought, has no protection against dissolving into slushy sentimentality or into a cruel oppression visited on those who fall out of the range of our standardized, 'natural' love responses."[19] The current spiritual restlessness and interest in religious movements or what is called spirituality can be either "slushy sentimentality" or a call for putting thinking as it informs believing into the context of piety.

One final observation. Study of the information-processing approach with its cognitive focus reminds one repeatedly of the importance of language. Language may be important to faith only through the believing component of faith, but to the degree that language is one of the essential components of being human, it can also be said that without language it is impossible for belief to fulfill many of its specific functions in human existence. To use one example, it was suggested earlier that one function is "to link lives of individuals and communities to larger, ultimate realities and purposes." (See Chapter 2, p. 20.) How can people communicate their perceptions of ultimate reality or think together about the Christian calling or make ethical decisions without the use of language? Further, as James Fowler says in his discussion of faith development, "unless we are part of a community that uses language in faithful ways, the reality that is mediated by language will be distorted."[20] Language, like thought and belief, contributes to the development of faith.

To say that thinking is an aspect of belief is not to say that it is all there is to belief. But it is to say that it is important, and that without understanding—which is sought by the thinking individual—believing is unlikely to make any difference.

6

BELIEVING
and PARTICIPATING
Group Interaction Models

Introduction

Beliefs, according to our thesis, are "sustained, reformed, and embodied by the faith community." That statement points to the social context of belief, as considered in chapter 3, and to a presupposition foundational for all approaches to teaching. "We flow together," Horace Bushnell says.[1] The unconscious influence of the faith community helps shape persons' beliefs and their very selfhood. But in a special way, this statement has importance for an approach to teaching dependent on groups and group interaction, as is the case with the second cluster of models. It gives attention to what happens to the person as he/she participates in the life of a group. How does *participation* relate to the teaching ministry, to that intentional activity directed toward belief formation? That is a question to be raised with respect to a consideration of "believing and participating."

When teaching is so conceived that it takes into account what is learned from the experience of being a part of a group, as well as from the thinking activities of the individual, it belongs to what Bruce Joyce and Marsha Weil call "social models of teaching," or what is called here "group interaction." It is even possible that thinking is more productive when it is sharpened and tested by one's peers, but the dimensions of learning related to this family have more to do with the "feeling" component of belief as it informs, enlivens, and personalizes thought. The interdependence of the cognitive and affective domains is captured by a comment after a group Bible study: "I cannot remember when my mind has been so actively engaged as when we were probing Bible passages and commentaries and quotations in our exploration tonight of the term 'the people of God.' But then when I suddenly realized that we in this room *are* 'the people of God' as we listen to one another, care for one another, are bound together by a common purpose bigger than any of us—*that* moment was when I *knew* what the term meant."

The comment might have come from a participant in one of Wesley's class meetings or societies. This approach, centering on participating, has behind it many influences. The social learning theory of religious educators like George Albert Coe, C. Ellis Nelson, Randolph C. Miller, John Westerhoff, and others has implications for teaching. John Dewey is as important to this second approach as he is to the information-processing cluster. He, along with George Albert Coe, had a vision of what could be contributed to society by persons who shared responsibility for learning, deciding, and acting. The T-group or encounter group, arising in the 1940s, has to do with developing interpersonal skills, both because of the contribution to the person and to society. What characterizes the teaching approach that draws on such influences as the ones mentioned here?

Characteristics

ROLE OF THE TEACHER:
  guide and resource person skilled in group process

ROLE OF THE LEARNER:
  initiator of ideas and procedures
  participant in cooperative investigation and decision making
  shared control and responsibility with the teacher

STRATEGIES:
  variety of strategies appropriate, depending on task or subject matter assigned or chosen by group
  planning, formulation of task, research and report
  simulation
  role-play
  evaluation (ordinarily, units of study would include periodic times of feedback or debriefing the process as well as the conceptual learning; thus evaluation becomes a learning strategy)

Because of the confluent educational orientation of this approach, it is hard to be precise as to its distinguishing marks. However, some generalizations can be made.

First, the community of faith presupposed as context for all teaching approaches and all belief formations becomes directly, functionally important when a microcosm of the life of that community becomes a matrix for learning. That is what happens in this family. Process and experienced reality move up alongside structure as factors contributing to learning.

Second, knowledge is *constructed* by persons in interaction with one another. It is not something "out there," not information to be processed and assimilated. It arises out of the ongoing and immediate experience of persons, interpreted in the light of their heritage and the interpreted experience of others. Because knowledge is so constructed, it emerges as meaning, and is appropriated as belief.

Third, motivation is less individualistic than in the information-processing family. Or as James Nelson says, personal motivations and incentives are much more intimately dependent upon "meaningful involvement in groups and communities" than is often assumed to be the case.[2] One could say further that the motivation which emerges out of group interaction is also a motivation to serve the welfare of others, of the group and of the larger community. Attention is to be given, therefore, to both individual and group, or to the interdependence of the becoming of the self with the integrity of the community.

Fourth, one cannot predict completely the outcome of teaching in any model in this family. In fact, Joyce and Weil say that those who value this approach "hope" that this will be the case. *"Those who emphasize democratic process hope that the outcome of any educational experience will not be completely predictable."*[3] When people bring and use their own perspectives, and seek to build their own unique frame of reference within a shared reality, something new may emerge. A group may agree on *how* it works or on *what* it will explore, or the teacher may specify both, but neither teacher nor student determines in advance precisely *where* the group will come out.

Fifth, the approach is to be directed as appropriate to all levels of both affective and cognitive domains. Nobody determines in advance what is to be the inner, personal level of response of participants, but occasionally, or even often, persons will be given an opportunity to say how they feel about what they have learned. That statement often becomes an act of commitment, and a guide to action.

Sixth, the teacher is one who should be skilled, knowledgeable, and mature enough personally to be able to shift roles as the group develops leadership skills. Insights and contributions from the group are welcomed. And the growing autonomy of a free and responsible group is a sign that the approach is achieving its purpose.

Illustrations

If a group (rather than an individual) were to work through Dewey's steps in thinking, then his *How We Think* could be combined with his *Democracy in Education,* and most of the basic assumptions of the Group Interaction Family of models would be available. The much-heralded case study method could easily be developed into a model. When a group in graduate school assumes the role of specific historical or theological scholars, engages in research, and participates in discussions centering around agreed-upon issues, the general principles of this approach are being enacted. There is a kind of identification process that takes place, where values as well as ideas of a scholar are assumed, and all participants can enter into an enriching process through which they move to their own conclusions. Like Steve Allen's television program, "Meeting of Minds," this approach opens up many levels of understanding. Other methods may be suggestive of this approach, even though they have not been formalized as models. Here, three models are described.

1. Group investigation. In a tenth grade Sunday School class, interrupting the beginning of a teacher's carefully planned information-processing lesson, a student interjects a question. "If a person does not believe in Jesus Christ, does he always go to hell when he dies?" The question seems serious. Other comments indicate that the question arises from the death of a school friend of most of the members, in a car accident the night before. He proclaimed himself an atheist, and had challenged the efforts to express belief by more than one member of the group.

What should be done? The teacher in question quickly abandoned plans, and began exploring concerns. Three "real" questions emerged: Is there a hell? If so, what is it? Do non-Christians all go to hell?

It is not hard to imagine the next steps. Plans were made for class members, in twos and threes, to investigate resources, conduct interviews, and do independent Bible study for a period of three weeks, with Sundays as work sessions together. Reports were finally brought in, conclusions formulated, unanswered questions listed, and the whole procedure evaluated.

What we have is a group investigation model, all the more lively because the "puzzlement" with which it ordinarily begins is genuine, arising from students. Sometimes, to move into this model, a teacher develops a situation which will evoke questions—a film, an open-ended story, a quotation. When the situation is explored and the study task formulated, the group organizes for work, does the investigation, reports, evaluates, and determines what has been accomplished and what is still to be done.

In her *Exploring the Bible with Children,* Dorothy Jean Furnish gives an account of introduction of a unit to fifth graders.[4] As children enter the room where their teachers are at work, they are faced with walls posted with pictures. The questions are: "See if you can figure out what our new unit of study is going to be about!" After a few minutes, as children talk, Rick blurts out, "It just looks to me like we're going to talk about everything in the whole world!" Rick is right. The unit is to be on God and his world. The next question is, "What would you like to find out about God and his world?" Thus the planning process begins.

Note that the teacher moves the group into the area to be investigated, a viable approach, although it is a contrast to the youth group cited here. Children move in to help determine what is to be studied as well as how it is to be approached. Various combinations of initiative on the part of the teacher and students are possible. The important thing is to begin with puzzlement, and move into planned investigation.

D. J. Furnish uses this illustration as a model of leadership, designated as group/team teaching. In categories used here, it illustrates a group investigation approach to teaching with fifth graders.

When a group works in a disciplined way, when members and teachers refuse to let each other get by with careless work or superficial thinking, when care is taken to move toward conclusions, even though they have a tentative nature with

unanswered problems, this model can be effective and useful in achieving its goals
—building knowledge and interpersonal skills.

2. *Simulation.* To conclude a unit on hunger, one group uses *Baldicer,* [5] a simulation game in which participants make decisions about use of the world's resources
and experience something of the interdependence of the world's economy. This
is, technically, a simulation. It is an accurate representation of a segment of
reality. Scores indicate shifts in resources and power, so that pressure increases
as decisions must be made. Debriefing in this game, as in most good simulation
games, invariably deals with personal values and skills, as well as with economic
facts and ethical principles. Participants build knowledge in an integrative fashion
as they become involved.

Ministers in a continuing education event engage in Bible study using a
dramatic biblical episode, "Job and His Friends."[6] In groups, persons study the
background and position of each of the biblical participants, then choose and
instruct representatives. All members of the group reassemble to hear the friends'
conversation with Job. The final interchange between Job and God is moving.
In debriefing, ministers talk about the new perceptions that came to them
through the process, the difference made in Bible study, their personal insights
about understanding of and relationship with God.

This procedure is, in a sense, a simulation, although a modified one. Probably
it is more role-play than simulation. Whatever it is called, the dramatic qualities
are involving, and its outcomes are those characteristic of models in the approach
under consideration.

There are three major phases as this model is developed:

Orientation and preparation—linking of what is going on to the bigger unit
of study, if necessary; rules interpreted and roles assumed; study or research carried out

Introduction and enactment of the simulation

Debriefing—often moving from "what did you feel in this role?" and "what
did we learn?" to the use of purposeful questions and interaction, relating
the particular simulation to the unit of study.

The teacher who introduces *Baldicer* with, "Let's have fun today with a
game" may throw the whole session off base. "Let's see what we would do if we
had opportunity to make decisions about the world's resources" should be better.
The role of the teacher is a critical one at every step—knowing when to let a
discussion carry itself, when to intervene with relevant information, when and
how to draw things to conclusions, when interest is still high.

3. *Depth Bible study.* Periodically there appears in church life an effort to help
people believe in their own ability to find meaning in the Bible, without dependence on presentation or interpretation by scholarly clergy. Only *after* people try

to hear the message for themselves do they turn to a resource person, as the teacher or the pastor, for help. There are at least three ways in which this is done.[7]

First, each member of the group agrees to read the selected Bible passage three or four times before the study group convenes, and to mark it with checks to designate an insight or area of agreement, and with question marks to designate points which are not understood, with which the person disagrees, or which he or she wishes to discuss. The group time consists of discussion of the checks and question marks. Sometimes they match; sometimes they are listed from all participants and then discussed. Comments are fed in by the teacher or by a resource person designated for the session after the initial discussion.

A second plan is for individuals to study independently, and either before the group meets or at the beginning of the session, for each person to put the passage into a brief summary statement in his or her own words. The group forms its own statement. The teacher serves as resource person, responding to questions that emerge, by bringing in contributions from commentaries. The group moves to the depth level with the question, "What does this mean for today?"

A third plan is for everybody to bring commentaries and different translations, list the questions at the beginning, and work through them with ideas from everyone. Sometimes each person paraphrases the passage at the end.

The term "depth" is probably misleading. *Any* study, Bible or otherwise, can achieve a depth level. The term is used here to emphasize the personal dimension of meaning sought through encounter with the Bible. Sometimes the plan is distorted by persons who misuse the emphasis on "the meaning for me" or "for us" or who force artificial answers, with a poor sense of timing. But at its best, the plan does encourage people to trust the power of the biblical message, and to trust themselves and the resources of the group. It gradually diminishes dependence on an authority like a teacher, and recaptures something of the Reformation emphasis on the intrinsic authority of Scripture itself.

What is suggested here is illustrative of ways the "mission" of this approach can be carried out. Many methods—discussions, listening teams preparing for a panel presentation and then reacting to it, all the group methods advocated for adult education—are potential contributions to the process being considered here. The test question is whether the methods are used intentionally, whether they contribute to the purposes of the approach in a way consistent with its underlying assumptions. One other exemplar of the approach might well be Thomas Groome's "Shared Praxis," considered in chapter 8. Placed in that chapter dealing with action and reflection because of Groome's emphasis on "praxis," following the influence of Paulo Freire, the model might just as appropriately have been considered here.

Reflections

With respect to belief formation, this particular approach to teaching has several advantages. One has to do with the fact that a person has the opportunity to sharpen and test beliefs against those of others. As the result of his research and reflection about belief, David Myers warns against a hothouse environment in a church school. To develop a "germ-free ideological environment" is to perpetuate the "image of the unchallenged Sunday School faith being over-whelmed when the small-town lad goes to the big university," with no practice in handling doubts or attacks on faith. The group interaction approach to teach-ing has a potential for carrying out Myers' recommendation:

> Christian educators concerned about nurturing a faith which will endure assault are therefore best advised to introduce belief-threatening material within a sup-portive context for examining it.[8]

Persons can remember their *own* interpretation or defense of an idea in a discussion with others, but they also modify their positions by picking up enlight-ening or relevant contributions from others.

Similarly, just as a person may come to know what he or she believes through articulation, there is added the "feeling" component through many activities frequently used in this approach—for example, in the simulation model dis-cussed, as well as in role-playing. When a person genuinely becomes involved in the role of the Prodigal Son, that person might be heard to say, "I have talked about forgiveness and grace before, but now I *believe* in them as realities because I feel as though I had experienced them."

In fact, the attention to group process characteristic of this approach to teaching provides opportunities for persons to develop skills in cognitive activi-ties, to "build" knowledge cooperatively, but also to build competence in inter-personal relations. The key to the learning that occurs is *participation,* bearing out Randolph Crump Miller's theory of education, with his emphasis on experi-ence and its interpretation. A final advantage is the wealth of teaching activities that fit this approach, those that facilitate interaction and can thus easily be incorporated into existing models, or can serve as the base from which one builds new models.

But, methodologically speaking, there are dangers. Just as the knowledgeable teacher can become engrossed in information-processing strategies and be cut off from "where students are," not even recognizing boredom when it occurs, so the teacher using group interaction strategies can be misled by the "busyness" into thinking something is being learned.

Or again, teaching is not the same thing as therapy—although certainly therapy can contribute to belief formation. Church groups can turn into discus-sions of personal experience or testimonials that induce momentary warmth and satisfaction, but eventually run into dead ends. In commenting on "sharing groups," Robert Leslie says, "almost every successful attempt at meaningful group life has involved study."[9] To achieve the potential of this approach to teaching, with respect to belief formation, the cognitive and affective domains are both involved in the interactive process.

In addition to the methodological comments, three other observations are in order, one theological, one sociological, and one pertaining to the person of the teacher.

Theologically, the doctrine of the priesthood of believers is important as a foundation stone for this approach to teaching. To hear and answer God's call is to become a part of a living organism, the church, the Body of Christ, and to be available to one another, not only in shared ideas, but in that ongoing support and care which is ministry. As we "put on our neighbor," to use Martin Luther's terminology, we become a priest to one another. Laity—and technically, that means the *whole* people of God, not just the non-clergy[10]—are not simply amateur assistants to the preacher. Laity are full participants in the development of those beliefs which link past and present, tradition and experience, in a shared, responsible activity through which meaning is appropriated as persons, together, struggle to understand. Selves are formed, de-formed, transformed, in that process, as Lewis Sherrill says.[11] Therefore, even in a small study group, *all* persons need to be aware of what it means to participate in "the priesthood of believers."

If the process of group interaction can relate experience and tradition, as proposed, so that beliefs become integrative factors, it is possible that the fragmentation of life observed by sociologists can at least begin to be overcome. Particularly if it is the case that the church often becomes a contributor to fragmentation, as Borhek and Curtis say, there is need to investigate the potential within this approach for overcoming that fragmentation. Intentional efforts to use it for that purpose are advisable.

Then, as for the teacher, there is opportunity to maximize the attitude of openness and conviction advocated by Thomas Green. In a sense, a teacher can model that attitude. *If* every member of a group has something to contribute, the time will come when the teacher will be requested to offer a judgment, a position—and a good teacher will know whether the timing is appropriate, whether the group is mature and responsible enough to keep thinking. Much is demanded of a teacher in this approach—not only willingness to make the very resources of his or her *being* available to persons, but also knowledge, interpersonal skills, sensitivity to timing, artistry in holding things together.

There is no more assurance that this approach to teaching will work than there is for any other, but surely, if belief is related to the community of faith, the interactive process considered here is a way to relate belief and faith.

7

BELIEVING
and ENCOUNTERING
Indirect Communication

Introduction

There is another dimension of believing, that of holding an idea as true. In a sense, this dimension has to do more with "being held" by that which is believed than with establishing an idea as other than or over against oneself. It has to do with risking, becoming involved, being open to change by that which engages the depths of the self. When one's whole being is confronted with Truth, then believing becomes a process of finding what is "the truth for *me*," as Kierkegaard would say. This dimension we shall call *encounter*. It has to do with insight, imagination, intuition, *gestalt.* The belief that may emerge from encounter has a richness and depth, a multi-faceted content, that surely must be related to what we mean when we speak of the person's being formed by that which is believed.

The approach to teaching most clearly connected with encounter is indirect communication. Storytelling, drama, visual art, television, and other such forms have the potential for communicating meaning not easily accessible otherwise. But there is no assurance that these indirect ways of communication will lead to encounter, just as there is no assurance that information-processing models of teaching will lead to thinking, or group interaction models will lead to participating. Perhaps uncertainty or risk is greatest with this approach, because of the nature of the communication intended. What, then, is this "indirect communication?"

Søren Kierkegaard, the great Danish philosopher-theologian-writer, is the name that first occurs when one thinks of indirect communication. He established the category which, technically, is so integrally part of his philosophy that it cannot be taken out of context and used here to define the way in which we shall use the term "indirect communication." But Kierkegaard's position can inform our approach. For him, Truth does not stand as an objective, abstract content which can be investigated directly. It cannot be analyzed, nor learned and then applied; it is not a result to be derived from immediate sensation and cognition. Nor is it resident within the individual in terms of moods and feelings. Rather, it is subjectivity. It comes into existence over and over again within a person, where the individual, with a kind of "double reflection," perceives the idea and simultaneously responds to it in a choice which is a recognition of concrete meaning, action, appropriation of that meaning. Truth thus has a personal quality. The individual comes to exist through it. With this kind of intention, Kierkegaard moves to indirect communication, where he uses myths, parables, poems, pseudonymous publications in which he explores various points of view. His attempt is to engage a person in enough ambiguity and puzzlement that the person's search for Truth leads to self-examination and decision. *That* is more important than content *per se.*

Jerome Bruner, already cited with respect to information-processing models of teaching, sees art as a way in which the human being is aided in a search for identity and a perception of reality. Better known for his cognitive theory, Bruner's awareness of the "left-handed" qualities of imagination, intuition, and feeling marks him as an educator who understands that to be human involves more than rationality, structure, or discipline. Although Kierkegaard's focus is on the religious sphere, where Bruner's is on a way of knowing that expands the whole concept of education, both are concerned with "the human condition." Both reject that kind of effort to know which has become "too aseptic and constrained."[1] Bruner affirms those "happy hunches and 'lucky' guesses . . . stirred into connective activity by the poet and the necromancer looking sidewise rather than directly."[2]

For Bruner, when students encounter appropriate art forms and are given freedom to respond, several things happen. Art which is genuine calls forth effort "to resolve the ambiguity that is a feature of works of art,"[3] and this entering into a "category of possibility" (strange, that Kierkegaard should use the same terminology) opens the door to the connecting of those "empty and lonely spaces between one's experiences."[4] One senses meaning through and behind one's varied responses. Or there is a "shock of recognition," the "fit" to experience where a concrete form points to generality.[5] Thus art becomes a mode of knowing "that defies the rational methods of the linguist and the psychologist," a mode of knowing through what may be called a "grammar of metaphor."[6]

Art, indirect communication *par excellence,* is sometimes evident in mass media, as in television productions. The official United States Catholic National Catechetical Directory asks for serious attention to the "capabilities and potentialities" of media.[7] Whether or not the medium qualifies as art, "catechists should be aware that a concept concretized in a medium is no longer simply an abstract idea but an event."[8] Sometimes what happens is not that a concept is concretized, but that a whole range of meaning is opened up to one through the event, an event which just may become an encounter with truth.

The current interest in "theology as story," and in educational use of storytelling, along with sporadic activities of the church in drama, interpretive dance, and arts festivals, suggests a readiness for consideration of indirect communication.

People respond to the kind of embodied truth found in art through many avenues and on many levels, and are thereby engaged personally in and with the truth.

Is this *teaching*—this use of indirect communication? Even if we respond to Thomas Green's view of teaching as raising questions of "why?" and "how?" in such a way that there is called forth a "manifestation of intelligence," it seems that the answer is *yes*. The way is less clear than with other approaches, but what could better call forth the question of "why?" than one of Jesus' parables or television's "Holocaust" or "Roots"? And the fact is that to employ indirect teaching is to view teaching as an art, and the teacher as artist.

Characteristics

ROLE OF THE TEACHER:
> artistic, imaginative use of art forms, with a sense of timing and appropriateness to students and subject matter
> a willingness to "stay out of the way," and not to prescribe response

ROLE OF THE LEARNER:
> to enter into, discover, and appropriate meaning for oneself
> to make the effort to perceive truth, and to risk decision and response

STRATEGIES:
> use of a variety of forms—parables, drama, film— "clothing" that which is to be communicated
> silence, introspection, free reflection and response
> expectation of personal encounter with truth and decision

Of the several qualifications or guidelines to be placed on this approach to teaching, one of the most important is best expressed negatively. The use of art for *direct* teaching is prohibited in the approach under consideration. There is a vast difference between indirect communication as explicated here, and the use of visual materials to decorate, illustrate, explain, clarify, or moralize. In *all* approaches to teaching, the demonstration, the visual aid, and the diagram are useful. But they are tools, used in such a way. Similarly, art criticism requires another approach to teaching. It may be preparation for later, fuller engagement with art, which "completes" it. Indirect communication is a different mode of knowing. Positively stated, art as related to indirect communication, according to Bruner, releases people from "forms of instrumental knowing." We move into a kind of thinking that "is more symphonic than logical."9

A second related point follows from Bruner's reference to re-creating and living that possibility glimpsed in the beholding of a work of art. What happens is that there may be set in motion a process which will eventuate in qualitative change in the self. If this possibility *is* characteristic of, or a hope for, indirect communication, it becomes obvious that "the goal . . . is not to clarify an idea, secure acceptance of a proposal, or arouse emotion, but to stimulate the recipient to independent activity."[10] Therefore, choosing that which is to be offered to the recipient is of the utmost importance, if it is to have shaping power on the individual.

A third characteristic has to do with the type of knowledge to be derived through indirect communication—inner, personal meaning. That meaning may be a relating of the particular and the general, of the individual and the universal. It may take the form of subjectivity, as described from Kierkegaard's perspective. Always it crosses the boundaries of the cognitive, affective, and psychomotor domains of learning considered here. It involves the will, the desire and struggle of the self to become. The wholistic nature of the encounter means its subjectivity is not so much a domain as a process of becoming for the self, or a relation between the self and the Truth.

This inner, personal meaning may well take the form of awareness of the connectedness of life. Kierkegaard's subjectivity has an ethico-religious dimension that is not necessarily characteristic of all indirect communication. What may happen is nearer to the yearning of the self for a unity of experience that overcomes the fragmentation of life. There is an integrative, synthesizing level of knowing. In T. S. Eliot's "still point of the turning world,"[11] past and future come together in the present moment. But the self is never absorbed into the object of art. Because that which is encountered is held at a little distance, it can evoke in the participant-recipient a kind of understanding that offers meaning.

Finally, just because indirect communication has to do with personal meaning, the teacher must be particularly alert to the learner's freedom. It is a matter of respecting the learner's uniqueness and independence, a refusal to use techniques of persuasion or influence that infringe upon the learner's right to choose, to decide. Raymond Anderson, interpreter of Kierkegaard, says that Kierkegaard admired Socrates' "way of holding the pupil at a little distance so as to preserve the learner's freedom."[12] Further, in contrast to a "fundamental disrespect for human personality," he sees that, when we are talking about the Kierkegaardian "leap," that is, "the choice which determines one's destiny," a person "has a right to risk his own life, but not that of another."[13] For Kierkegaard, as for Aquinas and Augustine, in the final analysis, God is the Teacher. What the human teacher does is to point toward the Truth in diverse, indirect ways, in a process which is never finished—and to vanish at the moment of truth.[14]

But then, it may be said that this is always what the true human teacher does. When we are thinking of inwardness, of subjectivity, the point becomes critical.

Illustrations

The category of indirect communication is one for which it is hard to find models of teaching. Joyce and Weil do not include it in their writings. Because it depends so largely on the intuition of the teacher, about the only thing one can do is to encourage the teacher to enrich her/his own life with all types of art, to "sense" where students are, and at appropriate moments to build in exposure to art, with the use of silence as well as free response.

For both teacher and student, it is possible to develop an environment when works of art are placed in a room, and changed from time to time, thus enabling connection with the truth conveyed. A unit can be ended with a time of engagement with a work of art in a period for response and reflection. Referring to stained glass windows, mosaics, sculptures, music, poetry, dance, the National Catechetical Directory says this: "From the very beginning, the church has used the arts to communicate Christ's message and fix it in people's minds and hearts."[15] What is being suggested has more to do with preparation of an environment than with planned teaching; nonetheless, the environment teaches, indirectly. This particular approach reminds us of that fact.

We are not including in this approach the *creating* of works of art. It is possible to make a case for including it here, but what happens in writing a poem or painting a picture seems nearer to the mission of the "personal" approach considered in the next chapter.

1. Some suggestive incidents. Two actual situations in which graduate theological students served as teachers in a class session are summarized here, selected out of dozens of possibilities where students experimented with indirect communication.

In interpreting Bruner's view of art as a mode of knowing, one teacher describes a man named Silas. There is information about height, weight, heritage and family, a two-sentence biographical statement. Then he reads an obituary, worded exactly like a current brief newspaper statement. Finally, he reads aloud Robert Frost's "The Death of the Hired Man." Silas, the broken man who suddenly reappears to "help ditch the meadow" is no longer a statistic. He is a particular individual who brings into the lives of the class the pathos and the dignity of human life and death.

In interpreting Kierkegaard's *Philosophical Fragments*, the teacher arranges the room with a row of chairs facing the windows, looking out on the trees and sunlight. Speaking from behind the group, she dramatically tells a story, one she has written. Plato's myth of the cave obviously has sparked the idea. People seem to enter into the experience on any one of many levels of awareness of the meaning of the Christian pilgrimage. At the end, people sit in silence for a time, and then leave.[16]

2. Kierkegaard's writing as indirect learning and teaching. Just as Dewey's *How We Think* serves as a major source for teaching approaches relating to cognitive processes, so Kierkegaard's writings serve as a frame of reference for indirect communication. Socrates had gone as far as human reason could go, according to Kierkegaard. But something was lacking—a level of understanding not available through the Socratic method, a perception of the nature of knowledge that did not necessarily deal with his own need "to understand my place in life, what God really wants me to do," or to "find the truth which is a truth for me."[17] What Kierkegaard undertook in pursuit of those concerns—really the question as to what it means to be a Christian—was to build on Socrates in a lifelong literary vocation. His productions taken together are an effort to help people find for themselves answers to similar questions, and to choose with a clear knowledge of what would be involved in the choice. His literature, by which he educated himself in the meaning of Christianity, is an unparalleled effort to delineate the subjectivity of the individual, from varying perspectives. This process of reflection and of personal appropriation was for Kierkegaard a lifelong process of becoming a Christian. It was his hope, not that he would be admired and the results of his reflection systematized and memorized, but that the individual whom he called "my reader" would join with him, existing in the reading as he himself had done in the writing, in the authors whom he had created, and thereby be caught up as a participant in that same process of becoming a Christian. Thus is set up a kind of "dialectic of education," according to Ronald J. Manheimer, whose *Kierkegaard as Educator* explores what he sees as an educational theory.

Kierkegaard seeks to reduplicate his own reflection in a variety of forms which portray "a movement of thought and language designed to enable the reader to make use of his own capabilities for appropriation."[18] A part of the educational theory demands of both writer and reader a "passion for honesty."

> Just as Socrates feared to be in error more than he feared death, so Kierkegaard feared most of all lest he should be found dishonestly to have appropriated a result that he had not earned through personal reflection, and tested in the fires of personal experience . . .[19]

Willingness to run risks is also required. For Kierkegaard, knowledge, in the sense of certainty, is never possible. But belief, not as a cognitive act but as a passionate "sense for becoming," runs the risk of committing itself. It is the opposite of doubt, which is fearful of "every conclusion that transcends immediate sensation and immediate cognition."[20] Because belief "believes the fact of becoming," it runs the risk that doubt cannot run. It is "a free act, an expression of will," affirming "the 'thus' of what has come into being."[21] Believing, like existing, is incomplete and always in process of developing.

Every teacher may not be able to find writers or other artists whose work will draw persons into encounter with truth through indirect means. In fact, in the latter part of his life, Kierkegaard turned to direct communication. But the teacher can become acquainted with the novelists, dramatists, and painters whose life contributions are in themselves indirectly dealing with ultimate meaning in such a way that those who see or hear may be drawn into the process. It is in fact the case that there are specific acts of indirect communication which communicate more clearly and powerfully than any direct presentation.

BELIEVING AND ENCOUNTERING: Indirect Communication

But probably the most important thing is the attitude found in Søren Kierkegaard, an attitude which could, potentially, bring into existence new, untried approaches to teaching.

3. The teaching vocation as "indirect communication." Is it not possible that the classroom teacher, in putting together models and approaches to teaching, drawing on both direct and indirect communication, may develop a form of teaching similar to Kierkegaard's literary production?

Joseph Axelrod, in *The University Teacher as Artist*, contrasts the didactic and the evocative modes of teaching.[22] The evocative, which engages the student in a process of inquiry and discovery, is nearer to artistry in teaching. Axelrod is not talking about indirect communication, but his suggestions about the evocative mode hold out the possibility of a teacher's viewing his/her vocation in its totality as a form of "indirect communication." What is involved here is not only the use of stories by the elementary teacher, or of the classic film "The Parable" by a youth teacher, or the replacement of a lecture on the resurrection by a combination of music and visual arts, but also the sequencing and timing of activities in an ongoing process where teacher and student alike are perceived as responding, unique individuals.

Reflections

Not every learner will be able to respond to indirect communication, but every learner, every human being, has a deep yearning for that kind of symphonic thinking or symphonic awareness of which Jerome Bruner speaks. One needs to have things "come together," to participate in meaning and yet to be aware of oneself as existing within that meaning. That kind of possibility is at the heart of indirect communication. It is a possibility which is not restricted to the world of art, although when it occurs through that world, or through other approaches to teaching, it is both a gift and an expression of a kind of expectancy on the part of both teacher and student. And if we are to reap the benefits of this approach, the same kind of careful preparation is necessary as for all other approaches, combined with willingness to nurture the imagination, and to experiment.

Those benefits are many. They are implicit in terms or ideas which have been used—connectedness of experience, belief which is a "sense for becoming," willingness to search for "a truth for *me.*" In these last years of the twentieth century, such benefits seem tremendously important. What is behind the "Born Again" movement, the emphasis on spirituality, the lack of passion for any cause? Why do so many people respond to the superficial manipulation of emotions with a shallow religious guise in the electronic church? Weaknesses in education are not the only culprits, of course, but there *are* hints in indirect communication as to *some* things that can be done educationally to help resolve some of the dilemmas we face, and they are contributions that come from education to other functions of the life of the church.

There is also a warning. The "Me" focus of this approach is needed, but the "We" concept of group interaction models is missing. Believing is not *only* a matter of "the single individual," as Kierkegaard often seems to suggest. It is that, but it is more. It involves reciprocity, receiving as well as giving, within and by the community. Kierkegaard was "inaccessible to true mutuality," according to Manheimer.[23] One should not try to destroy the distinction of the approach by trying to make it become "everything," but it is well to remember that other approaches are necessary to complement this one.

There is another whole area for reflection that can only be touched on here. People are being reshaped, turned into different creatures, by mass media. Roman Catholics officially express a concern that the wider church is not exploring the significance of this fact. The Directory speaks of media literacy, of the need to train media producers and media users.[24] Otherwise, in these times, catechesis cannot be carried on intelligently or effectively. Direct as well as indirect communication is involved in media, of course, but perhaps no area has more untapped potential nor more problems for education for these next years than has television. But that same thing can be said about indirect communication in general.

One final reflection. To the degree that faith itself has a "symphonic" quality, where everything, simply everything that is, comes into perspective, this indirect communication seems to have unique potential for the work of the church. Is it not, after all, the form of communication God chose in self-revelation through Jesus Christ?

8

BELIEVING
and BECOMING AWARE
Personal Development

Introduction

The kind of belief that is an "index" to faith rather than a mere "saying" is one that involves commitment, feeling, and conscious involvement of the self. The one who believes is aware that it is *I* who believe. I exist. I think, feel, act, will to be. Belief is not a matter of some objective statement to be arrived at and verified scientifically—or at least, it is not only that. There are intuitive moments of insight when I perceive that I am in touch with meaning hitherto inaccessible to me—meaning which brings heightened awareness of self, and often awareness of being constituted as a self by a transcendent reality who affirms my uniqueness.

Although intuition and feeling within the person are operative in other approaches to teaching, and personal meaning emerges from those approaches, the distinctive feature being considered in this approach to teaching is the development of the self and the self's "power to become," to use Lewis Sherrill's term. The fact that an infant can come to say "I" marks him/her as human. Eventually, even for an adult, that means the self can "go no further back" than to say, "I am," because "the self is an ultimate form of reality."[1] Marked by vitality, self-determination, self-consciousness, and self-transcendence, the self is *"both a being and a becoming."*[2] In his *The Gift of Power,* Sherrill presents the thesis that a Christian teaching ministry can help persons to receive the gift of power which enables persons to cope, and to become who they are called to be. In spite of all the writings of the 1970s and early 1980s on humanistic education, confluent education, sensitivity training, and the like, no church educator has written about the self with the eloquence and ability shown by Sherrill in this 1955 work. In fact, it seems newly appropriate for these last years of the twentieth century, in which people seem disoriented, without a sense of self or of destiny.

Sherrill's concern is not just with the growth of the self. He is clearly Calvinistic in his view that self-knowledge and knowledge of God are interdependent.[3] He is even more firmly biblical in his view that the Bible speaks to the deepest human concern, in a "predicament-theme" kind of dialogue which becomes an arena for revelation and response to effect the becoming of the self. Joyce and Weil's "personal models" share some of his assumptions, although Sherrill's wide range of theological concerns changes the focus. For Joyce and Weil, the focus of this family of models is "on the individual's construction of his or her own reality," on finding personal identity. "The individual's life validates itself—his or her unique existence and experiencing of life are what counts."[4] The goal for them is not so much short-term instructional effects as it is long-term nurture of the whole personality. For Sherrill, the goal is the development of an approach within the Christian community which can overcome the fragmentation of ministries rendered to persons, in the hope that the fragmentation of the self can better be overcome. At this point, Sherrill's view is close to what was said in the consideration of the context of belief, as he sets forth the need for both together-ness and separateness, for being "a part" and for being "a self."

What kind of teaching can contribute to that element of believing which we are calling "awareness"? Clearly, there is no one method that can easily bring about the internal perception we seek. That is, in a sense, a possible concomitant of all approaches we are considering. On the other hand, there are processes which can be set up and encouraged, as having the potential for stimulating self-awareness; encouraging persons to set up their own goals and pursue studies independently; planning for a summarizing-evaluating activity at the end of a unit of work, where students formulate their own position and "take a stand," as it were; offering the option of a personal response of a poem, a prayer, or a painting at key points in a study. There is the whole realm of creativity where a person brings into being something which gives form to meaning. This is the other side of indirect communication, when a person expresses the self in art, rather than responds to a work of art. Certain training programs help people learn to express and assert themselves with a resultant increase in a sense of power. Imagination is stimulated through metaphorical thinking, and new dimensions of self-con-sciousness open up. In fact, possibilities are limited only by the imagination, or by failure to be intentional in one's teaching.

What is the perspective from which one makes decisions about teaching that lead to becoming more aware of and in touch with one's own selfhood? For Sherrill, the perspective is that of life as a pilgrimage—rather than a treadmill or a saga—so the focus is on that pilgrimage, in a biblical context, rather than on the pilgrim in isolation.[5] For Edward Edinger, offering his version of basic Jungian categories, life is a process in which the human as a self-conscious individual emerges from a collective unconscious. That is, for Jung and for Edinger, the self does not come into being simply as a result of personal experi-ence and interaction with other selves. Rather, the "collective unconscious or archetypal psyche," called the Self, is the reality, the "wholeness" out of which the ego emerges and moves toward identity.[6] Some people say that the first part of life is that in which the ego separates from the Self; the last part, that in which the ego moves back into union with the Self. Edinger prefers to say that life has alternating rhythms in the relationship, and that life in its fullest meaning moves toward an appropriate "ego-Self axis," as "the vital connecting link between ego and Self that ensures the integrity of the ego."[7] What Sherrill and Edinger both are suggesting is that one does not promote the development of the self simply by focusing on self-awareness. Or they are saying that one does not simply see self-actualization in isolation. Theological and philosophical assumptions and commitments are expressed through the positions they take.

Characteristics

ROLE OF THE TEACHER:
  student advocate and guarantor
  facilitator
  resource person
  reflective counselor
  one who is knowledgeable about and appreciative of the arts, and of that
    which is imaginative and "actualizing" in the student

ROLE OF THE LEARNER:
  assume increasing control of and responsibility for his/her own learning
  express ideas, feelings, imagination, in growing personal freedom
  develop the capacity to feel, to be aware of self and others and the total
    environment, and to express oneself
  find ways to relate effectively to others

STRATEGIES:
  use metaphorical, lateral and/or divergent thinking
  participate in processes designed to increase self-understanding and build
    self-image
  develop individual learning contracts for both subject matter and procedures
  utilize role-playing and simulation

Three comments are offered here as suggested points for consideration by those planning to use this "personal" approach at some point in teaching. First of all, the teacher is indeed a critical element. Her/his attitude and expectations are more important than any one model or method. Is the student a "thou" to the teacher? A person cannot affirm himself/herself, cannot trust, cannot have the courage to risk expressing feelings or ideas, unless that person has been loved, trusted, affirmed, cared for. That fact has been stated so many times in so many ways that it is almost impossible to hear in all its depth and implications. And the teacher is one who is also "on pilgrimage," seeking to become an authentic human being.

There is another facet to the role of the teacher. There must be a kind of intuitive decision as to when it is appropriate to have a student write a poem instead of an analytical essay, or to insert a unit on awareness training (as a

technical model) in between one on concept formation and one on group investigation. That is one point at which the teacher functions as artist in the overall
purpose, sequence, and design set up for the teaching process.

A second point has to do with the student. Granted the assumption that each
individual is indeed unique, possessing gifts of personhood and vocation, and has
inner resources untapped by the present educational procedures, we can point to
the need for occasions in which a person is helped to become aware of self and
environment. Although we can never separate a person into compartments, as
in present-day "domains" or in earlier faculty psychology, we can offer ways of
tapping a person's motives, of making contact with the whole person, by making
initial contact with some facet of the personality. At this point we think particularly of feeling, of emotion, of the affective domain. That dimension is never
absent from any approach to teaching, of course. In fact, demanding cognitive
activities sometimes eventuate in intensive affective response, of excitement,
enthusiasm, awareness of competence to think clearly. But here we are talking
about a direct, substantial effort to find ways in which a person expresses feelings
and perceptions, and in the process moves to new levels of awareness of self and
environment.

A slightly different emphasis occurs when we think of fostering a person's
creativity. Too often we have sought convergent rather than divergent thinking,
have rewarded analytical rather than metaphorical thinking, have worked with
outlines rather than with images. Thus, as many writers are pointing out, in
studies of the brain in relation to education, and in studies of modes of consciousness,[8] we are failing to encourage the development of the whole self. Work is
needed on the development of creative imagination, giving persons time to brood,
to let the unconscious work in a kind of "wrestling of the spirit" in a relating of
fleeting images and ideas in some form that can be offered to others.

A third point, which has to do with strategies, is both a warning and an
encouragement to the teacher to design models and methods that "fit" particular
situations. Some church education materials focus so much on how one feels—
about a Bible story, about an ethical issue—that only a superficial level is touched.
In a sense, such a technique either functions to motivate interest in the subject,
or to set up the illusion that one is dealing with personal concerns. Such a
technique often exploits the person, or bypasses the important information-
processing that needs to precede or accompany the offering of personal judgments or feelings. That is the warning. The possibility of planning ways that are
"tailor-made" to enable persons to move out toward being free, functioning
individuals is where the challenge lies.

Illustrations

Three of the models included here come directly from *Models of Teaching.*[9]
They are described as they have functioned in situations in religious institutions.
Some other models, included in a behavioral family by Joyce and Weil, might

conceivably be included in this section, where clearly conceived, tested training strategies enable the teacher to aid students in developing specific skills which give more control over his/her life, and in that sense, focus on self-awareness. But the relation is indirect, and to include them would call for more analysis than is possible here.

1. Expressive activities. The first illustration is not a model, but a listing of activities which foster personal expression and thereby increase the possibility that one will come to say *"I* believe" because it is I who have found a way to give form to what I think and feel.

The scene is an art festival held in a church. Paintings and crafts are on display. A dance group gives an interpretation of the Prodigal Son. A musical group plays a composition that later becomes a kind of theme song of the youth group. A hymn, written by one of the members, is sung by the assembled company at closing time each evening, and then becomes a part of the worship in the church service on the following Sunday. Even had one not heard the conversations, a visitor would sense from the whole affair that people had become more in touch with themselves. Even though all art forms are not of an obvious religious content, most seem to offer some interpretation that is indeed a religious affirmation.

Take another situation. A group of theological students, meeting for an academic year with a cottage of teenage boys at a correctional center, work diligently to develop a sense of self-worth among the juvenile "offenders." One Sunday afternoon Tom, obviously a leader, says he is working on a play. He is encouraged; it becomes obvious that he is trying to find and express some meaning in the situation in which he finds himself. The play is written, practiced, and finally presented publicly in a visit by the cottage to the students' school. Awkward, hesitant, but deeply moving, the play brings a new perspective to the writer and actors, a new sense of what it means to be a human being, regardless of the setting, to the audience.

In a religion class at a private school, a student asks to do a color videotape on creation, rather than write a paper. In a church school class, when sixth graders write a litany to be used at a baptism, they talk about their own baptisms, and in the worship, obviously participate with a new feeling of being "special" and included. At a youth retreat, culminating a year's confirmation/commissioning class, each person reads his/her confession of faith. One person says, "It is as though for the first time I believe, because I have tried to say what I *myself* stand for." Some members of the class share excerpts from the journals they have kept during the year.

Other instances could be offered. All would point toward an active, initiating, expressive stance on the part of the student. Many would manifest creativity. None would be casual activities to fill up time.

2. Awareness training. In this model, Joyce and Weil specify only two phases as the strategy—planning the environment and activity directed toward the goal, and then reflecting on how participants felt within the situation. Two situations will illustrate.

In the first, students in a teaching team bring in equipment from a rental firm handling hospital equipment—a bed, wheelchairs, walkers. A blindfold is put on one person, and she is given a task to do. Another is instructed to sit in a wheelchair and prepare refreshments for visitors, while another person in a wheelchair is to make up a bed. The exercises last for only a short while, and participants are observed by an increasingly involved group. A sense of empathy based on understanding emerges. The awareness is not only of one's own feelings, but of the outlook of others living daily with restrictions that change their perceptions of themselves and others. Discussions by the group broaden the insights from individuals.

In the second, everyone in the class is requested not to eat breakfast. At 11:00 A.M., one group, selected by random choice, is served a delicious meal, while the remainder of the class watches. What happened in the discussion demonstrates the potential in this kind of approach. Awareness in this case was not only of pangs of hunger, not only of resentment toward the "haves" from the "have nots," but a new awareness of complexities of world economics and of what seem like hopeless situations. One person who had eaten says, "How do we live with feelings of guilt and the need for forgiveness?" There is a new dimension to the discussion that follows.

3. Non-directive. Here the student establishes learning goals, determines processes and resources for carrying them out, often writes a contract, and always ends up with self-evaluation. This is often characteristic of an "honors" course approach in universities, of an "individualized learning contract" approach in schools, including church schools. Carl Rogers, translating some of his counseling assumptions into implications for teaching, is a leading advocate of such an approach. One of his main concerns has been with graduate education, where adults are often kept within boundaries that inhibit their initiative and stifle development of their potential. When persons *are* encouraged to explore their own questions, to engage in self-initiated action, they move toward new perceptions of self, new insight, new confidence. Or at least, if they have mastered enough learning strategies, they feel new confidence. The educational system has not been strong on developing independent learners. And of course, learning styles do differ. This particular model is directed more toward active, independent learning styles than toward passive, dependent learners.

4. Synectics. The essence of the model developed by William Gordon, called synectics,[10] is metaphorical thinking. Its strength is the development of creativity, even in the way ordinary things are seen and done in everyday life. Metaphoric activity clearly draws on the emotional component of human perception, although not in isolation from the intellectual. In fact, according to Gordon, "hunches" function in science in much the same way as creativity functions in art. The richness of feelings and insight combines with generative thinking to produce new perceptions and expressions in what can become "an intensely personal experience."[11]

The strategy moves through various phases of describing a situation or object, of drawing analogies, of "becoming" the object, on through restating analogies in a kind of "compressed conflict" and then going back again to the original task. Procedures focus either on "making the familiar strange," or on "making the strange familiar." Both procedures point to needs in church education.

In one school, a youth group is asked, "How is a church like a car?" The object is to make strange the familiar concept of church. Answers are quick and illuminating. "A car needs to be going somewhere or it's useless." "If the driver doesn't know where to go, everybody becomes frustrated." "If you run out of gas, you're in a jam." "If a wheel comes off, you could have a wreck." Other phases of the model, worked through, end up with a totally different perception of the church.

A seminary student, in summer work, uses an adaptation of the model in an imaginative way. At a church picnic, sitting around tables after a good meal and some hymn-singing, each family or group is asked to complete this sentence: "The gospel is like _____ because it _____." Each table hears the statements, then selects two or three analogies to share with the whole group. With great delight on the part of everyone, the next Sunday, contributions are compiled and arranged into a reading by the student pastor, to be used as a part of the worship, where the sermon is on the meaning of the gospel. Unifying and involving benefits of the procedure are obvious. The statement is offered here.

> The gospel warms and brightens our lives like fire and sunshine. Like road-maps, streetlamps and lighthouses, it shows us our path and the way to go. Like electricity, the gospel lights up the world in a mysterious way.
> The gospel is our food and nourishment. It cleanses us as water does. The gospel works in our lives like a vacuum cleaner, collecting our problems, and like Drano, it unclogs our minds.
> We find support in the gospel, and in that way it is like a girdle. Like a zipper, the gospel holds things together; like an umbrella it protects us. In the gospel is security like a blanket or a quilt. The gospel orders our lives as a calendar does and like a tree it grows through the years.
> The gospel is many things to many persons. You and I know that like the ocean, the gospel holds treasures in its depths.[12]

Reflections

Does the kind of activity we have described here, given the goals and assumptions of this teaching approach, speak to some of the concerns evidenced in the exploration of Eastern religions, and in the emphasis on spirituality and spiritual discipline? Careful work is needed to answer that question, and to answer three others, equally baffling. All activities as described here took place in a "schooling setting." Is it possible to bring together within the "school" a focus that draws on all life's experiences, integrating and internalizing the meaning found there? If not, what kinds of settings or structures *can* do that? And how does worship, that act of devotion and commitment, function in such a way that awareness of self *and* awareness of God move together? In a way, unless that happens, deep human needs cannot be met, according to the position of Lewis Sherrill, with whom we began this chapter.

Another cluster of observations centers around educational endeavors to find ways to do "person-centered teaching." That term has not been used here deliberately, because of technical historical curriculum connotations, and because of the temptation to use it in a simplistic distinction that contrasts it with "subject-centered teaching." But we are talking about concerns related to that term, or that emphasis in teaching. "Experiential education," often contrasted with "traditional education" in a misleading way, has not been mentioned here either, partly because *all* approaches involve some kind of experience. Even thinking, real thinking, is an experience. But what has been described does draw largely, although not exclusively, on what is ordinarily called experiential education. Similarly, although this approach often involves innovative ideas, it certainly is not the exclusive domain of innovation. In any case, innovation for its own sake is not the beginning point for the planning of teaching. What we need to do is to approach the "homelessness of mind" that really exists as a kind of "homelessness of self" in a way that is not faddish, that recognizes the power of the emotion in the becoming of the self, and that has behind it the substantive thinking of people like Lewis Sherrill.

In a related area, consider the attention given to the development of consciousness, and to modes of consciousness. Robert Ornstein, in a brief overview of the history of psychology, says the original psychological question was, "What is consciousness?" However, because of the difficulty of finding access to that inner dynamism of consciousness, psychology moved through such schools as the mentalist, behavioristic, psychoanalytic, and humanistic, finally coming back to the question again. Much of what is read and heard, he says, is "bizarre and facile cosmic blather,"[13] but there are signs that we are moving to a new level of definition, perception, and research. Whether insights come from research on the two hemispheres of the brain, or from remarkable accounts of control even of bodily reactions by Eastern mystics, or on the Sufi-like wisdom that touches unexplored areas of Western consciousness, we need to be attentive and persistent in our reflections on where and how we need to move in church education. Just by virtue of our theological stance on the corporate nature of the church as a community of faith, the Body of Christ, we cannot condone the individualism which could emerge from improper use or overuse of this "personal" approach to teaching. Nor can we condone the imitative, superficial activities often utilized by the church. But then, neither can we ignore the longing of the person to be able to say "I."

What *can* be affirmed and held out as a vision is the power of the Spirit to transform lonely, searching individuals into persons who know who they are and what they are for.

9

BELIEVING
and DOING
Action/Reflection

The organization of this chapter is different from the preceding four. What needs to be said about believing and doing simply refuses to fit into the categories used there; it spills beyond teaching into education, and beyond that, into the even wider area of the church and its mission. And yet, if we continue to be serious about the question of how belief develops and functions in human existence, there is no way we can avoid consideration of "doing the truth." The thesis around which this book is built refers to the faith community, where beliefs are embodied—the community which serves as the context for intentional teaching. We are pushed to move into that arena for our analysis here.

Is "doing the truth" to be called teaching?

There seems to be little room for arguing whether it is appropriate to say we teach people to swim, to play tennis, to sing (as in church choirs), to act (as in church drama), or to become involved in action in numerous other activities. Those all involve physical or psychomotor skills which Thomas Green would include in many of the activities of teaching as training. They are forms of "doing."

But how does one include actual acts of effecting social justice as teaching —not motivating action, nor raising consciousness about issues, nor applying biblical mandates in verbal formulations, but *acting?* When one moves into the realm of moral issues, of Christian discipleship in the world, should the action itself be included as "planned" teaching? To set up opportunities for service in order to "learn" helpfulness, or to contrive experiences that exploit some persons in order to give students the impression they have performed some great act of service—this is the corruption of the concept of "doing the truth." It is appropriate to say that we learn or are educated by "doing the truth," but it is more questionable to say we shall teach by "doing." Unclear thinking has not helped the cause of teaching, nor of relating belief and behavior more effectively. What can be said about the situation that will help in understanding and planning for teaching?

Mission and structure of the church

Consider as a kind of case study the account of "the Church of the People" at St. Stephen's, as presented by Georgeann Wilcoxson in *Doing the Word.* [1]

Beginning with reference to the rich culture of the Appalachian people of
the Virginias, Kentucky, and Tennessee, then offering analysis of some of the
problems faced by those people, the account moves to a particular town and
church.

> In one such coal town, the deaconess nursed back to health the son of the
> company manager. In gratitude the father donated eleven acres, where Grace
> House was built to be used by the deaconess as a service center for the people.
> After the deaconess' death in 1968, there was little activity in Grace House or
> in St. Stephen's church building eleven miles down the mountain. A few groups,
> such as VISTA workers and welfare rights people, used the facilities for meetings
> in the early 1970s. In response to requests from these community groups, the
> denomination decided to renew activity in the area. After a few false starts, the
> congregation of St. Stephen's began meeting with their new minister, Don
> Prange.

Don Prange, influenced by Paulo Freire, Brazilian educator-philosopher,
worked to help the people relate the gospel to their situation, learning with them
and working to move toward "responsible freedom."

> Don's co-worker, Linda Johnson, is a young woman who returned to her home
> in the mountains after college with a commitment to remain a bicultural person,
> utilizing the skills of the dominant culture in behalf of her own people.
> Linda lives at Grace House with three other women—a social worker, a
> teacher, and a public health nurse. They formed a feminist support group and now
> meet regularly with five other women from the community in an effort to continue
> raising their consciousness through reflection on their own life experiences, shar-
> ing problems they face as women in the mountains, and sharing insights about
> solving these problems. They also learn from women from other cultures through
> reading alternative publications such as those of a feminist group in New York
> City. The learnings about women's struggles with another culture are adapted to
> their own lives.
> The Church of the People at St. Stephen's, as the congregation has named
> itself, supports the work of Grace House. Don and Linda meet at least weekly to
> reflect on their ministry. Although the number of actual church members is very
> small, at Grace House the church and community merge through their common
> activities to overcome the suffering resulting from poverty and efforts to survive
> in a culture that belittles mountain people.
> The worshiping congregation meets on Sunday morning for a combination
> of Sunday school, worship, action planning, and reflection time. At least five
> elements are included in their time together:
> 1. Reflection on why they are there
> 2. Praise, thanksgiving, prayers, singing
> 3. Hearing and talking about the word of God from scripture and from their own
>   experiences
> 4. Commitment—time for the offering and for discussing the meaning of their
>   commitment
> 5. Getting ready to go back into the world—discussion and making plans for
>   actions they will take during the week.
> The organizing constitution of the Church of the People at St. Stephen's was
> written through the process of the congregation's study of scripture and reflection

on why they are together. From time to time it is reviewed and discussed as part of the worship on Sunday mornings.

What we have here is a total restructuring of the life of a congregation. The constitution, in its purpose, states clearly the mission of St. Stephen's is "to witness to the Lordship of Jesus Christ in every area of life." Their concern is to relate "faith and life—belief and deed." Activities of the congregation are so interrelated and integrated that it would be hard to say where "teaching" takes place. But learning occurs everywhere. It would seem that we have a way of overcoming the fragmentation of the life of a congregation into different divisions and ministries, the concern of Lewis Sherrill, and the fragmentation of the lives of persons, the concern of Borhek and Curtis.

Such a case study will help many people recall other instances where a whole congregation has planned for itself a different way of structuring its life and mission. A new church in North Carolina, several years ago, in a "pilot project," organized itself into action groups, assuming that in planning, doing, and evaluation, education would take place. Worship occurred somewhat in the same fashion as at St. Stephen's. After several years, it became apparent that children were not becoming acquainted with Bible stories, names, and events in a way that developed adequate data or categories to use in mission, so they added a time of direct teaching for children up through sixth grade. The well-known Church of the Saviour in Washington is set up in mission groups. Both congregations function as house churches, where it is easier to interrelate study, action, and worship.

Basic Ecclesial Communities, originating in Latin American Roman Catholic parishes, function in much the same way. One statement of purpose reads in this way: The Church is perceived as

> the people who come together to consider the well-being of all, to be sensitive to the problems of others in order not to leave anyone all alone, to discover the other person's ideas, to discern the leading of the Holy Spirit in the people, to reflect on God's action, to resolve the difficulties of each person, to pray together and live the Gospel of our Lord Jesus Christ, and to attend to the problems of the neighborhood.[2]

These communities are spreading rapidly, still centering in the worship of large groups as they meet together, but causing a complete restructuring of the parish, and of the role of the priest. Problems still exist with finding ways to focus on action, but at least the intention is clear.

In other situations, major reorganization of the life of a congregation does not take place, but a gradual adaptation of parts of a program to needs of the community begins to occur. Serving lunch to transients in a community, resettling refugees, opening the doors of the fellowship hall to people with no place to sleep, and providing mattresses to be spread on the floor—these activities begin to push toward an inter-relation of service and reflection on the gospel. One church sets up a lifestyle study group, prepares guidelines, and neighborhood groups covenant with one another to work together in support and renewal of their commitment to be responsible stewards. In another situation, a study of public education moves into an organized effort to work for improvement of the whole system.

Notice the variety of ways in which action is related to the worship and work of a congregation, and the ways in which teaching moves in and out of action. Some suggestions can be offered as to ways in which teaching can be related to "doing," even in the most ordinary program conceivable.

Teachers and group members can be encouraged to follow through with action when a spark of interest or desire is evidenced, even to the point of dropping printed study materials and using scheduled time for planning, reflection, and evaluation.

Use of awareness-training models, or consciousness-raising groups can be encouraged, where they are consistent with the stated mission of a church.

Training in problem-solving, with a focus on analysis, planning, and evaluating skills can be offered, where it is evident they are needed and will be used. (Otherwise, empty exercise lessens the possibilities that people will be interested in action.)

Attention can be given to teaching families how to become an "action" group in their situations, or at least, how to be aware of the "doing the word" that occurs in their own budgeting, planning meals or vacations, living generally.

Ministers can be encouraged to give special attention to their work with committees, carrying out the necessary teaching to relate action to the gospel, and to help members know how to take hold of the task and carry it through to completion (thus avoiding one of the greatest barriers to involving a congregation in service or action).

In each of these cases, teaching is involved, either as a preparation for action, or as a way of relating action to learning, of linking word and deed. All have to do with attitudes, imagination, willingness to adapt, or ultimately, the intention to live out Christian responsibility.

Christian discipleship

What can be done by way of encouraging the individual Christian to deepen faith and clarify a belief by action? When we talk about knowing the truth by doing it, we move inevitably to the individual Christian, to the knowing self.

Symbolic action can be encouraged. Seminarians, talking together about the

Selma march during the turbulent years when whites joined with blacks in their
seeking of freedom, identify issues and possible results of a decision to fly to
Alabama. One person says, "I know that, if I go, I am taking a step that is a
symbolic act. I shall never be the same again if I do it." He was right. He went to
Selma. His perception became focused, his commitment could now be verbalized
more clearly, he could—had to, he said—join the march at home when he returned
from Selma. The life of a church can help a person prepare for response in such
cases, and support him/her in living out the implications of that symbolic act.

Vocation is a term that needs reclaiming, in the sense of basic calling. When
one's whole life is experienced as calling, then what one does in television studios,
offices, factories, or political offices is response to that calling. One is at the heart
of those places where injustice occurs, dishonesty runs rampant, and persons may
ignore it or may ease into similar practices, and decisions are made daily that
affect the lives of hundreds. Every injunction of the Old Testament prophets is
immediately applicable again. How can we help ourselves and others to see that
our whole lives are lived out as disciples? Work in the programs of the church,
its committees, with written statements and planned action—all these are important. But the everyday world is where the action is. The "scattered" church moves
in and out of the "gathered" church for support and guidance. Through the
dynamic of that rhythm, the truth is appropriated by Christian disciples.

Approaches in teaching

Granted that the Christian acts which test, validate, and internalize belief are
more parts of the total life of the congregation than of the specific teaching
function, what can be said about the most useful teaching approaches? Joyce and
Weil do not include a cluster of models related to the "doing" emphasis, although
it is apparent that certain models are quite useful in the overall strategy described
under "the mission and structure of the church." For example, awareness training
obviously could contribute at appropriate points to several of the illustrations
offered. So would group investigation, or various information-processing models.
However, there are at least two approaches that focus directly on action. They
may be suggestive as to other ways of working.

The first one is usually referred to as the action/reflection model. Technically,
it probably is not a model, but it does offer a general direction and guidelines for
developing strategies. More recently it has been referred to as a four-phase process
called AAAR, signifying Awareness, Analysis, Action, Reflection. One of the
clearest and most useful guides to this approach is quoted here.

> AWARENESS
> This part of the learning process is designed to increase an awareness and deeper
> understanding of:
> • God's intention and purpose for human life as expressed in the Christian gospel
> • Forces, powers, and structures in human life that either enhance or hinder the
> accomplishment of God's purpose

• The Christian's responsibility to be involved actively in God's loving, liberating, reconciling, and healing work in the world
• The human need to celebrate God's active presence in the world

ANALYSIS
If heightened awareness is to bring forth responsible Christian corporate and individual action, careful, disciplined analysis of issues and problems is necessary.
• Information must be gathered.
• All facets of the problem must be explored, especially the ways those personally involved perceive and are affected by the problems, as well as its underlying root causes.
• The problem must be restated according to the new information gained.
• Goals for appropriate action must be set and plans for action made.
• Possible consequences of these actions must be projected and tested against the values inherent in God's intention for humankind.

ACTION
Obviously heightened awareness and careful analysis and planning are meaningless unless action follows. Participation in corporate action, as well as individual action, is an essential element if significant changes are to result. Action consistent with the Christian ethic will vary according to the situation, capabilities, and commitment of the group, and the plans made by the group.
    Our actions should move toward one or more of the following:
• The removal or alleviation of the forces, powers, and structures in human society that violate or hinder God's will
• The rendering of service to those in need
• The public witnessing to biblical concepts of liberation, justice, and love
• Preserving the existence of positive social structures against the attack of those who would replace them with fewer human arrangements
    Whatever action is taken, however, must reflect the best efforts of the group to discern God's will and the humble recognition of our inability to do so adequately; therefore, all our actions are taken in faith.

REFLECTION
If we are to learn from our actions and grow in our ability to enflesh God's work in action, we must evaluate consequences of our actions from the biblical perspective. We should plan for theological reflection on the experience itself, seeking to test the ethical assumption of our perception of God's will on which the action was based. An important result of action is an increasing awareness of the complexities of issues, the intentions of God, God's presence in the world, and the nature of Christian responsibility for mission with God. Such reflection enables continuous reorientation of learners, both as individuals and in community. Thoughtful involvement in the awareness/analysis/action/reflection learning cycle can result in more effective action and an enrichment of worship as God is glorified, human inadequacies are confessed, hearts are opened to the guidance of the Spirit, and covenants are renewed for action in faith. This returns learners to the awareness portion of the spiral on a new and deeper level.[3]

A study group, mission group, Sunday school class, or another group interested in mission can intentionally use this process as a guide for teaching and learning. Teachers would sometimes be resource guides, sometimes information processors, sometimes discussion leaders, or, if they cannot fulfill all the needed roles, they can bring in other resource people. In most cases, of course, the learners themselves will be resources for one another, sharing their personal gifts of knowledge and skills for the good of all. They will be active, not passive learners, determining their own goals and procedures as well as being willing to be included in study and action. Possibly no designated teacher may be needed at all.

A group might begin at any point—with reflection on a contemporary parallel to a biblical situation, or with an individual's awareness of a problem, shared with others, so that no planned consciousness-raising activity is necessary. In any case, the group process is important here, and one would hope a task could be carried out with a feeling of accomplishment, and of gratitude for the privilege of responding to God's call through action.

The second approach is known as "Shared Praxis," a terminology popularized by Thomas Groome. Paulo Freire was quite influential in the early stages of Groome's work, and in that of many other educators as well. The key question posed by Freire in his *Pedagogy of the Oppressed* was "How do I name the world?" The oppressed Brazilian peasant, through a problem-posing dialogue process called "conscientization" by Freire, gradually became a free, responsible self through his/her self-conscious and intentional action. The knowledge that resulted might be called conative, with will and desire united in action that in turn developed the freedom of sense, power, and understanding. What Freire did for Brazil (he was expelled because of his success!) is most appropriate for similar cultural situations, although some educators have distorted his approach into a kind of "method" or technique that has no power because of different philosophical and cultural assumptions. What Groome has done is not to distort Freire's basic work, but rather to take the concept of *praxis*, give it his own definition, and develop a quite different approach that seems to "make sense" for the middle class (and perhaps others). Groome sets it forth as a specific teaching approach, useful in Sunday school, parochial school religion classes, and other educational settings.

For Groome, *praxis* is the term preferred to *practice*, in that it refers to "reflective action," or an interaction of theory and practice not clearly designated by one English word. What he means by "shared praxis" is this:

> Christian religious education by shared praxis can be described as *a group of Christians sharing in dialogue their critical reflection on present action in light of the Christian Story and its Vision toward the end of lived Christian faith.* [4]

The five "recognizable pedagogical movements" in that dialogue are briefly described by Groome.

> 1. The participants are invited to name their own activity concerning the topic for attention (present action).

2. They are invited to reflect on why they do what they do, and what the likely or intended consequences of their actions are (critical reflection).
3. The educator makes present to the group the Christian community Story concerning the topic at hand and the faith response it invites (Story and its Vision).
4. The participants are invited to appropriate the Story in their lives in a dialectic with their own stories (dialectic between Story and stories).
5. There is an opportunity to choose a personal faith response for the future (dialectic between Vision and visions).[5]

Numerous illustrations are offered in Groome's book. In a ninth grade unit on the Eucharist, the group is asked to begin, not with the definition, but with answering a question, such as "What does the Eucharist mean in your life?" In the second movement, participants trace the change in the role of the Eucharist in their lives, and, as the process of critical reflection intensifies, consider "What do you want the Eucharist to be in your life?" In the Christian community story and vision, the "most obviously catechetical movement in the process,"[6] Groome presents the Eucharist, its meaning, and the responsibility it places on receivers. He shows a film. In the fourth movement, discussion centers on the images and scenes that "jump out" from the film, with probing in the discussion to find out why. Finally, in the fifth movement, the ninth graders respond to the question, "How will I give 'Eucharist' to people?"

It will be apparent, even from such a condensed account, that there is much interaction between the biblical story and one's own story, between the biblical vision and one's intention to respond in ways more faithful than when the exercise began. Groome takes seriously John Dewey's idea of experience and reflection and of "the reconstruction of experience" as being at the center of education. Certainly there is constant interaction between tradition and experience. In many ways, one is reminded of "depth Bible study." There is great potential in the approach, but also a danger that can be found in "depth Bible study"—that one will force connections, or state an application or intention, in the last step. But in either case, dangers can be avoided when there is a good teacher.

Does "shared praxis" really belong in a section on "believing and doing"? Only in the sense that it focuses on relating belief to the becoming of the Christian disciple, with obedient action related to Christian tradition. The approach could just as appropriately have been placed in "group interaction models." Because Freire's work centers so much on the necessity of intentional action (usually political and economic), educators have somehow anticipated a similar emphasis in Groome. But the use of the term *praxis* means different things for the two men. What we have for Groome is a useful teaching model, to be added to the spectrum of possibilities from which we select according to our intentions in teaching, to be balanced off with other models offering different values.

Believing

Is it indeed the case, as claimed by some researchers, that there is a correlation between orthodoxy and prejudice? Rodney Stark and Charles Glock say "yes."[7] They also go beyond prejudice to talk about the relationship between belief and "ethicalism" in general.

> . . . ethicalism may provide a substitute for orthodoxy among some modern Christians. Ethicalism—the importance placed on "Loving thy neighbor" and "Doing good for others"—is more prevalent in denominations where orthodoxy is least common. . . . Furthermore, individual Christian church members whose religious beliefs are the least orthodox are slightly more inclined to score high on ethicalism than are the most orthodox. . . .[8]

Merton Strommen does not accept Glock's and Stark's conclusion, not only because he questions their methodology, but also because his own research points to the judgment that what makes the difference is *what* is believed. A gospel-oriented belief and value system does lead to love of neighbor. Strommen adds,

> There is no direct relationship between prejudice and the value dimension of a transcendental view of life. . . . The indirect relationship between prejudice and belief is that misbelief appropriates and shapes the content of orthodox belief for its own purposes of legitimizing hatred and violence.[9]

And in fact, Glock and Stark offer the assertion that "theology is the core of commitment; it tells us more about the character of an individual's religious behavior than does any other aspect of commitment."[10]

The picture is complex. When we deal with the relationship between believing and doing, we must think not only about *what* is believed, but about *how* it is believed—the intensity, the degree of commitment. Then there is the question of motivation, and of contradictory beliefs. James Nelson, affirming that "what we as Christians believe about God does indeed give shape and style to our moral action," concludes that such questions must be dealt with in relation to motivation.

> Thus, while I believe that God wills me to be a peacemaker, my motivation to act may be undercut by the belief that, after all, I am a powerless person. . . . Or, disturbed by the thought that certain peacemaking acts might threaten my personal comfort and security, I can simply give my own welfare higher moral priority than God's claim upon me as a peacemaker.[11]

The very fact that throughout history people keep developing different philosophical or scientific hypotheses about the relation between belief and behavior points to a kind of consensus, a conventional wisdom that leads us to say there *is* a connection. We cannot sort out all the complexities, but we can set up situations in which we examine the consistency of our stated beliefs and our actions, as well as the logical connection between the clusters of belief. In that examination, we can draw on the resources of our tradition, and we can develop the habit of "telling the truth in love," knowing that we need the help of one another in seeing ourselves. The group with whom we identify influences us, and if we identify with a company of Christian pilgrims, we may come to know through experience how belief and doing fit together.

10

PROSPECTS
for the FUTURE

A community, including a faith community, transmits its values and beliefs, transmits what it *is*. That fact was assumed as a starting point for this study. The question to be investigated, then, was whether and how teaching, as a ministry, could serve a more intentional function in that process—a question of particular importance because of the "homelessness of mind" which besets post-industrial human beings.

Both in analysis of some of the manifestations or causes of that "homelessness" and in the exploration of ideas about ways of effecting change, there is an implied hope that the future may emerge as a more focused expression of Christian faith. Perhaps even the tentative holding out of a vision of the authentic individual, one in whom word and deed are integrated around beliefs held with "openness and conviction" and a devotion to truth, will be a contribution to the future. Societies or communities need unifying images to which they give support in educational systems as well as through social influences. Suggestions offered about the nature of those communities and more specifically about approaches to teaching as they impinge upon believing may be useful to those who wish to help shape the future, rather than to be shaped by it in a defeated reactive way. What the "prospects" are will not be predicted, nor will prescriptions be offered. But a summary review of some pervasive themes from earlier chapters and some emerging hypotheses (or better, "hunches") about desirable directions, will be offered as a concluding statement.

Need for "conceptual goggles"

Analyzing the nature and function of Thomas Kuhn's "paradigms" and Stephen Toulmin's "conceptual framework," among other schema, Joseph Novak speaks of "conceptual goggles"[1] as those spectacles through which human beings see and process experience and ideas, and thus perceive order and meaning in life. What Novak says is quite consistent with the thesis of this book, as stated in the first chapter, and points to several assumptions functioning throughout this study.

That persons need "conceptual goggles" to cope with life, and more, to experience meaning as a sense of response to ultimate reality and ultimate purpose.

That one's conceptual inheritance, as Stephen Toulmin says, can be appropriated through the development of one's own frame of reference for understanding, and further, that the individual can make a contribution to humanity by participating in the ongoing evolving assessment and re-creation of both the conceptual inheritance and his/her own perceptual system. (John Dewey's comment that "genuine communication" produces "a community of thought and purpose" between an individual and the race[2] illumines the point.)

That conceptual inheritance, or beliefs and belief systems, makes no sense at all apart from a particular historical community, with its story, symbols, habitual ways of thinking and doing. That is to say, beliefs cannot be perceived as logical systems in isolation from lived reality. Nor is ideology to be viewed in the negative sense of ideas developed as weapons or rationalizations for use by individuals or societies for selfish ends. Rather, ideology is viewed positively, as the humble, heuristic, intentional effort to make sense of things.

That in recent years, inadequate attention has been given by the church in its teaching ministry to helping people develop beliefs in such a way that they will speak to the situations described. Or, to put it positively, a rethinking of teaching in relationship to belief formation may be a useful contribution to individuals and the society at this moment in history, because belief is inevitably related to faith, to moral action, to the becoming of the self.

What this last assumption suggests is that there is a need for "conceptual goggles" to be worn by those responsible for the church's planning and programs. But most of the book is actually an effort to make a contribution to a discussion of how *teaching* can be conceived of as an aid to belief formation, with some beginning possibilities for enactment of that perspective. Consider briefly what has been said or implied about teaching.

Teaching as limited, as focused, as potential

In order to promote cognitive clarity, distinction is to be made among concepts of schooling, education, socialization, and teaching—not because those terms are unrelated, but because they are not synonymous, and indiscriminate comparison of the terms promotes little more than fuzziness of thought. Teaching is used here to refer to those planned occasions in which designated teachers set up a process and structure for dealing with subject matter in such a way as to enable students to assess the truth of the same in terms of their own frame of reference.[3] In some approaches, teaching occurs at intervals in an ongoing, more comprehensive process, as in the action/reflection model. Subject matter is more than static concepts. Truth is more than that to which intellectual assent is given. It is also that reality that is known through participation and doing. In any case, teaching is only one function, one activity among many, that contributes to the development of belief. It cannot be viewed out of context; therefore reference has been made to agencies and activities other than teaching. But no claim is made here that teaching is "the answer" for our troubled age, nor that it is more than a way of taking hold of the situation—albeit an important way. (The assumption that *any* one function of the life of the church provides "the" answer is likely to be both self-serving and idolatrous.)

The central point or organizing principle suggested here with reference to teaching is the conviction that it should be *intentional.* People who function from the perspective that there is a best way to teach, or who put together methods —even in a skillful way—without clarity about what they are trying to do and why, are not likely to make much contribution to the development of beliefs and belief systems that have the characteristics and functions described in this study. The models described by Bruce Joyce and Marsha Weil offer a way to begin being intentional. As those authors say, the classification into families of models can serve as intellectual tools for making decisions about purpose, subject matter, methods, learning styles, all facets of teaching. One does not begin by making a decision with reference to some nebulous "best" way to teach.

The clusters of models or approaches offered here are intended to be a first step toward making decisions about teaching within the community of faith, when one gets to the actual process itself. If one clarifies his/her own assumptions, and moves toward intentionality in teaching, that should bring a needed focus.

What can be said about the potential in teaching? Note that the question has to do with teaching generally, not with a specific approach to teaching. But at this point, the reader will already have formulated a tentative response to the directions and boundaries for teaching proposed here, and related it to what has already been done, or to what will later be tested through experience. But when one thinks of teaching, and the long history of the church's teaching ministry— Locke Bowman calls it "the church's first ministry"[4]—or of the image of the rabbi, it becomes evident that there is an ongoing vitality in teaching which moves toward the fulfillment of its own potential.

Attention has been directed here more toward *how* beliefs are held than toward *what* is believed. The second is needed, but much help in that area already exists. If a person really becomes open to an idea or an author's thought, that person runs the risk of being changed by engagement with the content. What we are doing here is looking at how the believer processes that engagement. One study book for adults, *Believing,* by Urban Holmes and John Westerhoff, helps persons become alert to the activity of believing.[5] Obviously, the teacher should be concerned with both the what and the how of believing, with having a belief system herself/himself, and knowing when and how and whether to share that belief, as a part of the process of helping others develop their "owned beliefs."

What about those occasions in which teaching does not "work," those anguished moments after a class when the teacher experiences only a sense of personal failure? When Brother Deogratias wrote Augustine, apologizing for imposing on the busy bishop, he received an encouraging reply, telling him not to be uneasy because he felt he did a sorry job. Probably "your own words sounded to you unworthy of others' ears only because you were longing to give your hearers something better." Reflecting on his own experience, on those moments of insight when cognition has flooded his mind "as it were with a sudden blaze of light," Augustine contrasted the inward joy he often felt in preparation with his sadness when "my tongue has failed to do my heart justice."[6]

The practical helps Augustine offered Deogratias would be helpful to us today. He even suggested that, if one wanted to learn what he, Augustine, knew about teaching, the best thing to do would be to watch and reflect on his teaching, rather than read what he had dictated. He recognized that "the hearers will mutually influence each other by their mere presence," and affirmed the eloquence of "the yearning heart." Augustine saw and helps us see the potential in teaching, a potential not easily developed, but one that is to be sought through "discourses true rather than eloquent."[7]

Dialogue

When one thinks of the teacher or of a phrase like "the yearning heart," one must ask a question. When one is committed to helping persons find and be able to live by "the truth for me," when intentional teaching is clearly conceptualized and carefully planned, what is it that happens between teacher and student? The "relatedness" that, for Martin Buber, is dialogue, surrounds and penetrates all approaches to teaching. Buber speaks of the child who, at night, alone in the darkness, is "invulnerable" because of the awareness of the presence of the mother. Thus the child is "clad in the silver mail of trust."[8] The situation is similar in teaching.

> Trust, trust in the world, because this human being exists—that is the most inward achievement of the relation in education. Because this human being exists, meaninglessness, however hard pressed you are by it, cannot be the real truth. Because this human being exists, in the darkness the light lies hidden, in fear salvation, and in the callousness of one's fellow-men the great Love.[9]

The teacher must be "really there." Teaching takes place in a context of mutuality. Dialogue is therefore not a method, but an attitude appropriate for all teaching—it can occur when no word is spoken, so certainly it does not refer to discussion. It is, in fact, the dynamic reality that comes into being in the I-thou relationship. For teacher as well as for student, it is a gift of grace.

"Rendezvous with disaster"

Move once more behind assumptions and views of teaching for belief formation to the world context. True, there is need for meaning and integrity in personal human existence, a point at which belief makes a difference. But what about the moral crisis facing humankind? What about nations devouring and polluting the world's resources, population growing faster than food supply, massive military spending picking up money saved from cuts in social benefits as the world rushes toward the possibility of nuclear disaster? All these concerns and others are listed by Norman Cousins in an editorial in *Saturday Review.* [10] We seem to be moving toward a world of anarchy where freedom is "becoming theoretical," he says. As for the life of the mind, we "may be drifting toward a world in which creativity has to struggle to breathe." Thus it seems to Cousins that the "rendezvous with destiny" foreseen by President Roosevelt and cited by President Reagan may rather be a "rendezvous with disaster."[11]

Hundreds of persons could be quoted to point to the possibility of impending doom for "the planet Earth" and all its peoples. That point is made here because, in the final analysis, it may be the prime reason for being concerned about belief. Individual meaning, yes—but what about obedience? Faithfulness? One needs to know what kind of "conceptual goggles" can be most helpful in working with others toward responsible action in the issues that face us. How do we receive and act on and reformulate our conceptual inheritance so that we serve with God in the world?

Numerous writers are putting the notes of understanding and morality in context.[12] The addition here, of thinking about teaching in relation to belief formation, is to be understood as one possible small action to be taken in responding to the urgency of the situation in which we live.

The idea of truth

What we are talking about here is not a tightly knit, logical system of belief, not a static body of propositions that may pose as absolute truth, not even truth that is experienced and "known" through intuition or mystical moments of awareness. What is meant, rather, is the idea of truth, and how it functions in our lives. Truth is before us as mystery, reality, and the wonder of that which is transcendent, which stands as reference, corrective, and source of power to those who seek to be conformed unto it.

And when we think of teaching, that is the reference point—truth itself. Belief in truth, though we do not possess it, constrains us, and propels us to continue seeking honestly, faithfully. If we become discouraged and uncertain as to whether what we believe is true, what can we say? Herbert H. Farmer helped students and "seekers" in his day, and his conclusion is still useful to us:

If a belief (1) shines in its own light with a certain inherent compellingness, (2) "works" in the sense both of satisfying our nature and of helping in the practical task of managing our world, (3) reveals on examination both internal consistencies and external harmony with other experience and knowledge, then we have in regard to it as full an assurance of truth as it is possible for a human mind to have and as it ought ever to ask.[13]

Those core beliefs (not too many of them) feeding out through interrelated clusters of beliefs are the channels through which we work with truth, and allow ourselves to be constituted by it.

For Wilfred Cantwell Smith, if conceptualizing is to be involved at all, if it is to be *"faithful,"* it must be "the *closest approximation to the truth of which one's mind is capable.* "[14] In a religiously plural world, we respect and learn from other persons and their efforts to be faithful in conceptualization, he says. The approach is *not* one of comparative beliefs, but rather of understanding particular beliefs in historical and cultural contexts—and being enriched by that understanding. Truth is far greater than any one person's perception of it, or than the combination of all perceptions. And so when one thinks of Ultimate Truth, or for the Christian, of God as revealed through Jesus Christ, the response can only be one of awe. For Smith, "faith is a saying 'Yes!' to truth."[15] Constitutive believing merges with faith "to set one's heart," and links believing and being —both the possibility of our "being" at all, and our relationship with Being

Notes

Chapter 1

1. James 3:1 (Revised Standard Version).
2. "Education in the Church," *Colloquy*, December 1973, p. 9.
3. (Richmond, Virginia: John Knox Press, 1967), p. 10.
4. Ibid., p. 190.
5. Volume II: *In Search of the Divine Centre*, trans. Gilbert Highet (New York: Oxford University Press, 1943), p. 18.
6. Ibid., p. 5.
7. Ibid., p. 9.
8. Ibid., pp. 9–10.
9. Ibid., p. 11.
10. (Toronto: University of Toronto Press, 1980), p. 10.
11. Ibid., p. 225.
12. Ibid., p. 242.
13. Polanyi, Michael and Harry Prosch, *Meaning* (Chicago: The University of Chicago Press, 1975), p. 180.
14. *Moral Nexus: Ethics of Christian Identity and Community* (Philadelphia: The Westminster Press, 1971), p. 11.
15. (New York: Random House, 1973), pp. 184–185.
16. *A Sociology of Belief* (New York: John Wiley & Sons, 1975), p. 176. Additional indication of the growth of concern about the "believing" activity of humans comes from the new "The Church's Teaching Series." See Urban T. Holmes III and John H. Westerhoff III, *Christian Believing* (New York: The Seabury Press, 1979).
17. *Beyond Belief* (New York: Harper & Row, Publishers, 1970), p. xix.
18. Ibid.
19. Unpublished paper, "Defining Religious Belief and Beliefs Today," 1978, pp. 4–7. Used by permission of Search, Inc., for whom the paper was written.
20. *The Leadership Passion: A Psychology of Ideology* (San Francisco: Jossey-Bass Publishers, 1977), p. 3.
21. The quotations in this paragraph come from Hannah Arendt, *The Life of the Mind*. Volume One/*Thinking* (New York: Harcourt Brace Jovanovich, 1971, 1977), pp. 3–6. Volume Two/*Willing* (New York: Harcourt Brace Jovanovich, 1978) continues investigations of the ideas introduced in Volume One.
22. Referred to by Martin Marty in *A Nation of Behavers* (Chicago: University of Chicago Press, 1976), p. 46.
23. See Wilfred Cantwell Smith's interpretation in his *Belief and History* (Charlottesville: University Press of Virginia, 1977), p. 41.
24. *The Life of the Mind*. Volume Two/*Willing*, p. 113.
25. One helpful analytical overview is given in Charles Y. Glock and Robert N. Bellah, eds., *The New Religious Consciousness* (Berkeley: University of California Press, 1976).

26. *Creeds of the Churches* (Garden City, New York: Doubleday & Company, Inc., 1963), p. 1.
27. Ibid.
28. Cf. Hannah Arendt's comment about Etienne Gilson who, in his *The Spirit of Medieval Philosophy*, spoke of philosophy as the handmaid of faith. Pope Gregory IX warned the University of Paris that the "handmaid might become the mistress," anticipating Luther's "fulminant attacks on this . . . folly, by more than two hundred years." *Willing*, p. 113.
29. *God in Search of Man. A Philosophy of Judaism* (New York: Farrar, Straus & Geroux, 1955), p. 34.
30. Hannah Arendt, *Thinking*, p. 141.
31. *The Creeds of Christendom*, Vol. I, *The History of Creeds* (New York: Harper & Brothers, Publishers, 1877), I. 204.
32. *Beyond Belief*, p. 67.
33. *Signposts for the Future* (Garden City, New York: Doubleday & Company, Inc., 1978), p. 5.

Chapter 2

1. (London: George Allen & Unwin LTD, 1969), p. 19.
2. Rodney Needham, *Belief, Language, and Experience* (Oxford: Basil Blackwell, 1972), pp. 41ff. See also Wilfred Cantwell Smith, op. cit., pp. 41–46.
3. P. v.
4. P. 78.
5. *Beliefs, Attitudes and Values* (San Francisco: Jossey-Bass, 1968).
6. Untitled, unpublished paper, March, 1978. Used by permission of Search, Inc., for whom the paper was written.
7. Ibid., p. 4.
8. Ibid., p. 10.
9. Ibid., pp. 8–9.
10. From *The Activities of Teaching* by Thomas F. Green, p. 53. Copyright © 1971 by McGraw-Hill Book Company. Used with the permission of McGraw-Hill Book Company.
11. Ibid.
12. See ibid., pp. 41ff.
13. Ibid., p. 47.
14. Ibid., p. 48.
15. Ibid., p. 53.
16. Ibid.
17. Op. cit., pp. 1–14, 57–58.
18. Borhek and Curtis, op. cit., p. 5.
19. Ibid., p. 23.
20. Ibid., p. ix.
21. Merton P. Strommen, ed. (New York: Hawthorn Books, Inc., 1971), Part IV.
22. (New York: The Seabury Press, Inc., 1975), p. 16, n. 13.
23. (New York: Harper & Row, 1978), p. 74.
24. Cf. D. H. van Daalen, " 'Faith' According to Paul," *The Expository Times* 87 (975–76), pp. 83–85; and Alan Richardson, ed., *A Theological Word Book of the Bible* (New York: The Macmillan Company, 1956), pp. 75–76.
25. Op. cit., pp. 43ff.

26. Ibid., pp. 64ff.
27. "Defining Religious Belief and Beliefs Today," p. 7.
28. P. 99.
29. Eleventh grade class at St. Catherine's, Richmond, Va., taught by Lisa Matthews. Videotape used by the author in classes at Union Theological Seminary, Richmond.
30. See interpretation in Merton P. Strommen, ed., op. cit., pp. 26–32.
31. Op. cit., p. 21.
32. (New York: Harper & Brothers, 1961), especially chapters 4–6.
33. *Institutes of the Christian Religion,* trans. Henry Beveridge, 2 vols., (London: James Clarke & Co., 1949), Bk. III, chap. vi, par. 4.
34. *Thinking,* p. 188.
35. (Chicago: University of Chicago Press, 1975), p. 69. All three quotes are from the same page.
36. See discussion of this point in Hans Barth, *Truth and Ideology,* trans. Frederic Litge (Berkeley: University of California Press, 1976), pp. 179ff.

Chapter 3

1. Op. cit., p. 8.
2. Ibid. Cf. pp. 59–83.
3. *A Rumor of Angels* (Garden City, New York: Doubleday & Company, Inc., 1969), pp. 42–43.
4. Volume I: *The Collective Use and Evolution of Concepts* (Princeton, New Jersey: Princeton University Press, 1972), p. 35.
5. Ibid., pp. 39–40.
6. Miller has written a large number of books explicating this idea. See Boardman W. Kathan, "Bibliography: The Words of Randolph Crump Miller," in *Process and Relationship,* eds. Iris V. Cully and Kendig Brubaker Cully (Birmingham, Alabama: Religious Education Press, 1978), pp. 124–133. For summary of Miller's thought see Sara Little, "Randolph Crump Miller: Theologian-Educator," *Religious Education* Special Edition September-October 1978, pp. S-67-S-77.
7. Many people are referring to this invisible, individual kind of religion. One source is the "electric church," to which, Martin Marty says, people can belong by carrying a radio or TV with them on a trip. Being "born again" may be selecting the favorite electric church hero. "The Invisible Religion," *Presbyterian Survey,* May 1979, p. 13. Reprinted from *The Lutheran Standard.*
8. Hart M. Nelsen, *et al.,* "A Test of Yinger's Measure of Non-Doctrinal Religion: Implications for Invisible Religion as a Belief System," and Richard Machalek and Michael Martin, " 'Invisible' Religions: Some Preliminary Evidence," *Journal for the Scientific Study of Religion,* September 1976.
9. "The Futures of American Religious Education," Marvin Taylor, ed., *Foundations for Christian Education in an Era of Change* (Nashville: Abingdon, 1976), pp. 16–17.
10. Ibid.
11. Borhek and Curtis, op. cit., p. 176.
12. Ibid.
13. Timothy J. Teylor, "The Brain Sciences: An Introduction," in *Education and the Brain,* eds. Jeanne S. Chall and Allan F. Mirsky (Chicago: The University of Chicago Press, 1978), p. 27.
14. Ibid.
15. Ibid., p. 30.

16. Three handbooks specifying objectives for each domain are widely used in educational circles: Benjamin S. Bloom, ed., *Taxonomy of Educational Objectives, Handbook I: Cognitive Domain* (New York: David McKay Company, Inc., 1956); David R. Krathwohl, Benjamin S. Bloom, and Bertram B. Masia, *Taxonomy of Educational Objectives, Handbook II: Affective Domain* (New York: David McKay Company, Inc., 1964); Anita J. Harrow, *Taxonomy of the Psychomotor Domain* (New York: David McKay Company, Inc., 1972).

17. One of the best overviews is the chart to be found in Jim Fowler and Sam Keen, *Life Maps: Conversations on the Journey of Faith*, ed. Jerome Berryman (Waco, Texas: Word Books, Publishers, 1978), pp. 27–33, 96–99.

18. *Will Our Children Have Faith?* (New York: The Seabury Press, 1976), pp. 89–91.

19. The writer first heard this statement many years ago in an address by Albert van den Heuvel, "The Heresy of Youth Work." He was then a staff member of the World Council of Churches. David Myers makes practically the same statement in his *The Human Puzzle*, p. 92.

20. Op. cit., p. 95.

21. Ibid., p. 103.

22. Ibid., p. 92.

23. Ibid., p. 126.

24. Merton P. Strommen, *Five Cries of Youth* (New York: Harper & Row, 1974), p. 65.

25. "A New Look at the Literacy Campaign in Cuba," *Harvard Educational Review* (August 1978), p. 34. Copyright © 1978, by President and Fellows of Harvard College.

26. Ibid., pp. 344–345.

27. Ibid., p. 344.

28. Fernando Cardenal and Valerie Miller, "Nicaragua 1980: The Battle of the ABC's," *Harvard Educational Review* (February 1981), p. 1. Copyright © 1981, by President and Fellows of Harvard College.

29. (Washington, DC: Publications Office, United States Catholic Conference, 1971), p. 23.

30. Ibid., p. 25.

31. "Understanding and Religious Education," in *Process and Relationship*, p. 43.

32. Ibid., p. 44.

33. Eigil Pederson, Therese Annette Faucher, and William W. Eaton, "A New Perspective on the Effects of First Grade Teachers on Children's Subsequent Adult Status," *Harvard Educational Review* (February 1978), pp. 1–31. Copyright © 1978, by President and Fellows of Harvard College.

34. *Truth.* Volume II, Questions 10–20 of *De veritate*, trans. James V. McGlynn (Chicago: Henry Regnery Company, 1953), p. 85.

35. Ibid., p. 83.

Chapter 4

1. *Religion in America, 1981* (Princeton, New Jersey: Gallup Organization, Inc., and The Princeton Religion Research Center, 1981), p. 38. Reprinted with permission of the Princeton Research Center, Inc.

2. Ibid., p. 77.

3. See tables on membership and attendance, ibid., pp. 24–36; p. 11. For 1978 figures, see p. 38.

4. *Religion in America, 1979–80* (Princeton, New Jersey: Princeton Religion Research Center, 1980), pp. 17, 20, 23.

5. Ibid., pp. 67–68.
6. Ibid., p. 63.
7. Ibid., p. 64.
8. Ibid., p. 1.
9. With Milo L. Brekke, Ralph C. Underwager, Arthur L. Johnson, *A Study of Generations* (Minneapolis: Augsburg, 1972), p. 287.
10. From *The Activities of Teaching* by Thomas F. Green, p. 55. Copyright © 1971 by McGraw-Hill Book Company. Used with the permission of McGraw-Hill Book Company.
11. Ibid., p. 202.
12. *The Intentional Teacher: Controller, Manager, Helper* (Monterey, California: Brooks/Cole, division of Wadsworth Publishing Co., Inc., 1977), p. ix.
13. Ibid., p. 96.
14. *Handbook I: Cognitive Domain.*
15. *Classroom Questions: What Kinds?* (New York: Harper & Row, 1966), pp. 3, 19–74.
16. Cf. Jerome S. Bruner, *The Process of Education* (Cambridge: Harvard University Press, 1962), p. 48.
17. *Handbook II: Affective Domain.*
18. Second Edition (Englewood Cliffs, New Jersey: Prentice-Hall, Inc., 1980), p. 1.
19. Cf. ibid., Chapter 1, "Against Dogmatism: Alternative Models of Teaching."

Chapter 5

1. Ernest R. Hilgard and Gordon H. Bower, *Theories of Learning* (Englewood Cliffs, New Jersey: Prentice-Hall, Inc., Fourth Ed., 1975). See Chapter 13, "Information-Processing Theories of Behavior."
2. Ibid., p. 436.
3. *How We Think* (Boston: D. C. Heath & Co., Publishers, 1910), p. 58. Reprinted with the permission of the Center for Dewey Studies, Southern Illinois University at Carbondale.
4. Ibid., p. 6.
5. Ibid., p. 116.
6. Ibid., p. 203.
7. Joseph D. Novak, *A Theory of Education* (Ithaca: Cornell University Press, 1977). See especially Novak's interpretation of Ausubel's "assimilation learning theory," pp. 71–80.
8. Joyce and Weil, op. cit., p. 77.
9. Ibid., see chart pp. 50–52.
10. *Teaching: the inside story* (Philadelphia: Board of Christian Education, The United Presbyterian Church U.S.A., 1967), p. 50.
11. Ibid., p. 53.
12. (Atlanta: John Knox Press, 1978), p. 1.
13. Ibid., Unit Preface.
14. Ibid., p. 7.
15. Ibid., p. 2.
16. Ibid.
17. Plato, *Protagoras and Meno,* trans. W. K. C. Guthrie (Baltimore, Maryland: Penguin Books, 1956), p. 128.
18. *How We Think,* p. 141.
19. *The Process of Thinking* (New York: David McKay Company, Inc., 1977), p. xii.
20. *Life Maps,* p. 19.

Chapter 6

1. Quoted in James B. Nelson, *Moral Nexus* (Philadelphia: The Westminster Press, 1971), p. 11.
2. Ibid., p. 13.
3. *Models of Teaching,* p. 224.
4. (Nashville: Abingdon Press, 1975), p. 118.
5. Georgeann Wilcoxson (Atlanta: John Knox Press, 1970).
6. Donald E. Miller, Graydon F. Snyder, and Robert W. Neff, *Using Biblical Simulations* (Valley Forge: Judson Press, 1973), pp. 117–134.
7. See fuller discussion in Sara Little, *Learning Together in the Christian Fellowship* (Richmond: John Knox Press, 1956), pp. 65–76, and E. H. Robertson, *Take and Read* (Richmond: John Knox Press, 1961).
8. *The Human Puzzle,* p. 108.
9. *Sharing Groups in the Church* (Nashville: Abingdon Press, 1970), p. 32.
10. Cf. Hendrik Kraemer, *A Theology of the Laity* (Philadelphia: The Westminster Press, 1958), pp. 50–52.
11. *The Gift of Power* (New York: The Macmillan Company, 1955), p. 45.

Chapter 7

1. Jerome S. Bruner, *On Knowing* (Cambridge, Massachusetts: Harvard University Press, 1964), p. 4.
2. Ibid.
3. Ibid., p. 67.
4. Ibid., p. 60.
5. Ibid., p. 72.
6. Ibid., p. 74.
7. *Sharing the Light of Faith* (United States Catholic Conference, Department of Education, 1973), p. 154.
8. Ibid., p. 155.
9. *On Knowing,* pp. 72–73.
10. Raymond E. Anderson, "Kierkegaard's Theory of Communication," *Speech Monographs* Vol. XXX, No. 1 (March 1963), p. 7.
11. *Four Quartets* (New York: Harcourt, Brace and Company, 1943), p. 5.
12. Op. cit., p. 10.
13. Ibid., p. 5.
14. Cf. Ronald J. Manheimer, "Socrates Vanishing: The Passion of Subjectivity," Ch. 2 in *Kierkegaard as Educator* (Berkeley: Univesity of California Press, 1977).
15. *Sharing the Light of Faith,* p. 249.
16. See accounts in Sara Little, "Ways of Knowing: An Approach to Teaching About Teaching," in *Process and Relationship,* eds. Iris V. Cully and Kendig Brubaker Cully (Birmingham, Alabama: Religious Education Press, 1978), pp. 15–21.
17. Quoted in David F. Swenson, *Something About Kierkegaard* (Minneapolis: Augsburg Publishing House, Rev. Ed. 1945), p. 10.
18. Manheimer, op. cit., p. xi.
19. David Swenson, Introduction to Eduard Geismar, *Lectures on the Religious Thought of Søren Kierkegaard* (Minneapolis: Augsburg Publishing House, 1937), p. xii.
20. *Philosophical Fragments,* trans. David F. Swenson (Princeton: Princeton University Press, 1936), p. 69.

21. Ibid., p. 68.
22. (San Francisco: Jossey-Bass Publishers, 1973), Chapter 1, esp. p. 12.
23. Op. cit., p. 204.
24. *Sharing the Light of Faith,* p. 157.

Chapter 8

1. *The Gift of Power* (New York: The Macmillan Company, 1955), p. 14.
2. Ibid.
3. Ibid., p. 17.
4. Op. cit., p. 146.
5. See the perspective interpreted in *The Struggle of the Soul* (New York: The Macmillan Company, 1955).
6. *Ego and Archetype* (New York: Penguin Books, 1972), pp. 3–4.
7. Ibid., p. 6.
8. Cf. Robert E. Ornstein, *The Psychology of Consciousness* (New York: Harcourt Brace Jovanovich, Inc., Second Ed. 1977), and Jeanne S. Chall and Allan F. Mirsky, eds., *Education and the Brain* (Chicago: The University of Chicago Press, 1978).
9. See pp. 133–217.
10. See his *The Metaphorical Way of Learning and Knowing* (Cambridge, Massachusetts: Synectics Education Systems, Second Ed. 1970), and the chapter on Synectics in *Models of Teaching,* pp. 165–186.
11. Joyce and Weil, op. cit., p. 167.
12. From worship service in Salem Presbyterian Church, Salem, Virginia, June 19, 1977. Used by permission of Mary Elisabeth Goin.
13. Op. cit., p. vii.

Chapter 9

1. Reprinted from *Doing the Word—A Manual for Christian Education: Shared Approaches* by Georgeann Wilcoxson, pp. 16–17. Copyright 1977 by United Church Press. Used by permission.
2. J. L. Libano, "A Community with a New Image," *International Review of Mission* (Vol. LXVIII, No. 271, July 1979), p. 246. See also Sergio Torres and John Eagleson, eds., *The Challenge of Basic Christian Communities* (Maryknoll, New York: Orbis Books, 1981).
3. Wilcoxson, op. cit., p. 22.
4. *Christian Religious Education* (San Francisco: Harper & Row, Publishers, 1980), p. 184.
5. Ibid., pp. 207–208.
6. Ibid., p. 214.
7. *Christian Beliefs and Anti-Semitism* (New York: Harper, 1966). See also James E. Dittes, "Religion, Prejudice and Personality," in *Research on Religious Development.* The "authoritarian" or the "closed-minded" personality is more likely to be prejudiced than is the "open-minded."
8. Volume One, *Patterns of Religious Commitment* (Berkeley: University of California Press, 1968), p. 217.
9. Strommen, Brekke, Underwager, and Johnson, op. cit., p. 292.
10. Op. cit., p. 179.
11. *Moral Nexus* (Philadelphia: Westminster, 1971), p. 17.

Chapter 10

1. Op. cit., p. 22.
2. *How We Think,* p. 224.
3. An adaptation by the author and Neely McCarter of Thomas Green's definition of teaching, *The Activities of Teaching,* p. 103.
4. *Teaching Today: The Church's First Ministry* (Philadelphia: The Westminster Press, 1980). Bowman is one of the twentieth-century writer-teachers who has contributed most directly to improving the effectiveness of teaching in the church.
5. (New York: The Seabury Press, 1979).
6. Aurelius Augustine, "The Catechizing of the Uninstructed," quoted in Kendig Brubaker Cully, ed., *Basic Writings in Christian Education* (Philadelphia: The Westminster Press, 1960), p. 65.
7. Ibid., pp. 71–73.
8. "Education," in *Between Man and Man,* trans. Ronald Gregor Smith (Boston: Beacon Press, 1947), p. 98.
9. Ibid.
10. Editorial, "Report to the Readers," August 1981, p. 6.
11. Ibid.
12. People like Hannah Arendt, Donald Evans, James Nelson, and others are mentioned throughout this study.
13. *Towards Belief in God* (New York: The Macmillan Co., 1943, p. 28.
14. *Faith and Belief* (Princeton, New Jersey: Princeton University Press, 1979), p. 168.
15. Ibid., p. 163.

Index of Subjects and Names